THE
POSITION
OF THE WORKER
IN AMERICAN
SOCIETY,
1865-1896

AMERICAN HISTORICAL SOURCES SERIES:
Research and Interpretation

LORMAN RATNER, Editor

PRENTICE-HALL INTERNATIONAL, INC., *London*
PRENTICE-HALL OF AUSTRALIA PTY. LTD., *Sydney*
PRENTICE-HALL OF CANADA LTD., *Toronto*
PRENTICE-HALL OF INDIA PRIVATE LTD., *New Delhi*
PRENTICE-HALL OF JAPAN, INC., *Tokyo*

Irwin Yellowitz
The City College
The City University of New York

THE
POSITION
OF THE WORKER
IN AMERICAN
SOCIETY,
1865-1896

Prentice-Hall, Inc., Englewood Cliffs, New Jersey

To Barbara

Current printing (last digit):
10 9 8 7 6 5 4 3 2 1

© 1969 by PRENTICE-HALL, INC.
Englewood Cliffs, New Jersey

Library of Congress Catalog Card No.: 71–86522

Printed in the United States of America
P: 13–676478–9, C: 13–676486–X

EDITOR'S FOREWORD

The Position of the Worker in American Society, 1865–1896 is a volume in the American Historical Sources Series, a series devoted to the process of interpreting historical evidence. The introduction to each volume will be followed by some of the original documents used to prepare the essay. Readers are thus invited to share the experience of turning raw evidence into history. The essay has been written especially for this series and is a contribution to historical knowledge as well as a demonstration in the writing of history based on sources included in this work.

American workers have been described as a conservative labor force that has accepted capitalism, rejected class identification, and generally looked to collective bargaining, rather than political action, as the means to better their condition. But why were these workers willing to accept such a system?

In this study, Irwin Yellowitz describes workers' commitment to the Protestant Ethic—the traditional American belief that hard work and good habits will result in the individual moving from wage-earner to entrepreneur. Even when such movement was rare, as it was in the decades under consideration, the belief in mobility persisted. The beliefs of an earlier era continued even when the realities of the world no longer supported them.

But American workers reacted in different ways to new conditions and traditional beliefs. Although most native-born workers continued to accept these beliefs, some recognized the contradiction between beliefs and reality and sought to reconcile the two. Among immigrant workers, some accepted—and even had held in their native lands—the belief in the success ethic. When these workers failed to succeed in America, a surprising number of them returned to Europe to pursue success there. Other immigrant workers remained in America and, like many native-born workers, became reconciled to their position as wage-earners. A few from each group became radicals.

These developments significantly influenced the American labor movement. Labor leaders also had to face the traditional American emphasis on individual mobility, and they had to reconcile the success ethic and the objectives of unionism. This fundamental problem produced sharp divisions within the labor movement concerning present policy and future prospects. It raised the basic issues, from which tactics and programs would emerge.

Professor Yellowitz has studied the American worker in terms of that worker's view of the society in which he lived and has considered the society's view of the working man. The author has grasped the significance of the interrelation of the two, which provides us with valuable insights into the nature of each.

LORMAN RATNER

Herbert H. Lehman College
The City University of New York

CONTENTS

The Position of the Worker in American Society,
1865–1896, 1

The Position of the Worker
in American Society, 1865-1896

The idea of America as the land of opportunity has surely been one of the strongest elements in this nation's self-image. During the nineteenth century, American spokesmen took pleasure in reminding Europeans that here achievement was limited only by ability and determination. Unlike their European counterparts, American workers were not part of a fixed class with little hope of upward mobility in the future. Instead, the American success ethic postulated freedom of opportunity and a fluid class structure, which meant an open path upward for men of talent and energy. Labor provided a route into the prosperous, independent, and highly regarded business classes, since a worker's trade could be the first step toward self-employment. Thus, the American worker was exposed to a success ethic which tried to win his allegiance for the capitalist system by promising him a share of its fruits.

This essay examines the character of the success ethic. It focuses on the reaction of American workers to the ethic during the final third of the nineteenth century. Did the success formula influence the behavior of workingmen in significant ways? In answering this question, we must examine the newly arrived worker as well as the native-born and those immigrants who had been in the United States for some years. Did these workers accept the mobility theme of the success ethic, or did they develop their own aspirations and objectives?

Naturally the reaction of workingmen to the success theme had a strong influence on the character of the American labor movement.

1

Labor leaders disagreed on the fundamental issues of what the position of the worker was in nineteenth-century America, and of what it was likely to become. We will examine the efforts of labor unions and their leaders to create programs, tactics, and organizations that would best serve the interests of American workers. By 1890, the direction to be followed emerged as labor leaders hesitantly turned from the older ideal of the success ethic to a new emphasis on collective action to win gains for workers who would probably remain workers. Labor leaders accepted this conclusion slowly, and in the 1880's it still faced stiff opposition from within labor's own ranks. It remained to be seen whether trade unions could convince the mass of the workingmen that their progress had to come through collective action within labor organizations rather than by the isolated efforts of individuals in search of the mobility proposed by the success ethic.

A similar development occurred among that diverse group of social critics and reformers who hoped to solve the "labor question." They also had to decide what the actual position of the worker was, and what course promised to meet his needs best in the future. Divisions occurred among these reformers, just as they did among labor leaders, over the crucial question of how relevant the success ethic was to the American worker. In the 1860's, many social critics believed that the success ethic was viable, and they hoped for an eventual end to the wage system; by 1890, it was clear that support was growing for the use of legislation to meet the problems that now seemed connected with a relatively fixed working class.

Clearly Americans were significantly influenced by a national creed that extolled the United States as the freest and most open community in history, that regarded the accumulation of wealth as the mark of progress, and that assumed that each man had an equal opportunity to advance in wealth and status. We will examine how this creed influenced the behavior of workingmen, labor leaders, and reformers, so that it may become clearer how their decisions and policies depended upon their view of the position of the worker in American society.

II

The most basic characteristic of American attitudes toward the position of the worker was the attempt to harmonize his situation with a system of free enterprise capitalism. There is no doubt that the success ethic of the nineteenth century accomplished this quite well (Source 1). Joseph Buchanan, a leader of the Knights of Labor, wrote that as a youth in Hannibal, Missouri, during the 1870's he "knew nothing of a 'labor problem.' In fact there wasn't any labor question as we understand it now, outside of the large cities and industrial centers."[1] Even within these industrial centers many accepted the conclusions offered over and over by the intellectual, political, religious, and economic leaders that "we are literally all workingmen." Men were equal in the opportunity for success, and this sanctioned the unequal results of that struggle. The ingredients for success were a time-honored mixture of frontier and Calvinistic virtues, with the stress on hard work, honestly done. It was assumed that such labors, combined with frugality and good sense, would provide the savings necessary for investment in business. Success lay within each man, and he need only strive for it in order to have access to the riches of the nation. Of course, other individuals would be seeking similar goals, and thus competition would decide who were the worthy ones.

Horatio Alger's stories extolled the success ethic, and even though Alger added the ingredient of luck to the dedicated efforts of deserving young men, good fortune always came to those who earned it. The imprint of a basic Christian belief in the rewards of the good life, linked to economic success through the Calvinistic version of the calling, can be clearly seen in the success ethic.

The success ethic was truly the corollary of the basic American political beliefs of the nineteenth century. The equality that argued for a democratic suffrage based upon the right of men to vote, rather than the de facto democracy of the colonial period based upon the ease of securing land, also called for an equality of opportunity in the economic area. The respect for personal liberties engraved in the Bill of Rights went hand in hand with economic liberties that demanded equal consideration.

The objective of all, and the accomplishment of those who were successful, was to move from the ranks of the craftsmen or industrial workers into the more select group of businessmen. Great riches was never the prime objective, and the success ethic recognized that only a

---

[1] Joseph Buchanan, *The Story of a Labor Agitator* (New York: The Outlook Company, 1903), p. 4.

few could ever become fabulously wealthy; instead the goal was escape from a wage-earning position—in which a man's earnings, and the very opportunity to work, were set by an employer—to a self-employed position where accomplishment would be determined by the talent and vision of each man. The journeyman worker might be little different in skill from his employer, but as long as he remained a workingman, his horizons were limited and his opportunities few. As a small business-man, he had the chance to earn substantial profits and perhaps, ulti-mately, considerable wealth; but he was also independent of all other men, and the success ethic fastened on this characteristic as much as on wealth itself. A man had been successful if he could call his liveli-hood his own, his house his own, his opinions his own. Dependence was as unfortunate in the settled economy of an eastern town as it was on the frontier.

If equal opportunity were offered, then those who failed had to look within themselves for the source of their poor fortune. The re-quirements for success were not education, capital, or family, but the acquired traits of fortitude, diligence, and frugality. Thus the poor should not point to their environment, but instead should seek for the weaknesses in character that led them to fail.

This conclusion was a great comfort to the successful and the wealthy, for it made poverty a justifiable situation. Charitable societies aimed to rekindle the flame of self-help that all men could acquire, and this was certainly cheaper than supporting the paupers on a dole. The poor were exhorted to stop spending money on liquor and other idle amusements, to shun the vices offered in every workingman's neighbor-hood, and, above all, to emulate the successful. To aid even the less inventive, success manuals of every level of sophistication charted the course.

Failure was not fatal unless the individual gave up the quest for success. This became the most heinous of all personal weaknesses. It opened the individual to scorn and condemnation, and, should he give up steady work, led to his exclusion from society. The success ethic called on men to overcome failure, to try all the harder, and to demand even more of themselves. The weapons would remain the same, but the individual must overcome the obstacles.

It has been suggested that a similar attitude pervades modern

American society. Repeated frustrations in efforts to follow the socially sanctioned road to success may lead to criminal activities that can provide an exit from an immobile lower-class situation. The nineteenth-century success ethic naturally rejected crime or immoral activity, but then, as now, the evidence of success rapidly became the external mark of it: wealth. By the late nineteenth century, men extolled wealth more and more, and the virtues that supposedly led to it less and less. In effect, no questions were asked about how this wealth had been gained. The dignity of labor seemed compromised, the status of the skilled worker degraded, while the indolent rich received the esteem of society. As the editor of *The Railway Conductor* pointed out in 1890, honest labor had been pronounced blessed by Jesus himself, yet it was now scorned in favor of "the individual who never earned a dollar in his life in an honest manner; the one who inherited all his wealth, never adding a penny thereto unless at the expense of others." Equally despicable was "the man or men who live and profit at the expense of others; the ones who 'sow not, neither do they reap,' yet wax rich because they impoverish the poor man." [2]

This same praise of labor, and hostility to great wealth, was to appear in the agrarian movements of the 1890's. The "producing class" included those whose labor brought visible results, but not the parasitic capitalists who did no obvious work, created no apparent product, fashioned no item, grew no crop, yet accumulated unheard-of riches. Henry Demarest Lloyd and other reformers spoke of a unity of the farmer and worker, and the producing class was a basic element in such plans. Of course, the alliance never came to fruition, for the producing class was divided within itself. The interests of farmers and industrial workingmen were often quite distinct and opposite. Moreover, the skilled workers feared the unskilled and semi-skilled, whom they viewed as competitors ready to take their jobs.

Representatives of the workingmen also attacked the increasing status offered white-collar occupations in comparison with skilled labor, since it obviously was based upon a hierarchy of status within a fixed working class composed of manual and nonmanual employees. The success ethic had traditionally granted dignity to manual labor. By hard

[2] "The Dignity of Labor," *The Railway Conductor,* VII (May 1890), 362–63.

work, one proved his ability to advance up the economic ladder. Skilled labor, in particular, had been regarded more as a step toward the position of employer than as a permanent situation. The skilled worker thus objected to any hardening of class lines, as well as to any loss of his status in comparison with other classes of employees (Sources 2 and 3).

The success ethic was rooted in a basic mutuality of interest between capital and labor. Abraham Lincoln stated the prevailing attitude very well in March 1864:

> Capital has its rights which are as worthy of protection as any other rights. Nor is it denied that there is, and probably always will be, a relation between capital and labor, producing mutual benefits. . . . Property is the fruit of labor, property is desirable; is a positive good in the world. That some should be rich shows that others may become rich; and, hence is just encouragement to industry and enterprise. Let not him who is houseless pull down the house of another, but let him labor diligently and build one for himself; thus by example assuring that his own shall be safe from violence when built.[3]

William Graham Sumner argued in a similar fashion that as the millionaire acquired his fortune, he helped each man to increase his own income. The American capitalist system thus linked the most modest shopkeeper and the aspiring worker with the men of great wealth through the mechanism of a highly mobile society. The difference among men was in degree, not kind, and the structure and operation of capitalism served the interests of all and allowed each man to achieve his fortune.

Although Americans might talk of an identity of interest, there most certainly was no identity of sentiment. Though fixed classes were denied, attitudes of class superiority were common. Thus those who had succeeded were prepared to grant the right of access to persons from lower classes, but they denigrated the poor until they had proven their character and ability through accomplishment. The poorer elements of the population were often characterized as "low and degraded" or "grossly ignorant," and it became clear that little was owed to the

---

[3] *Iron Platform Extra,* No. 40 (March 1864), 1.

poor since they had created nothing. The poor deserved their poverty and so deserved the reproach of the middle class; the only escape for the hard-pressed wage earner was to enter the middle class himself.

The strength and pervasiveness of the success ethic derived from both example and argument. Surely men could point to individuals who had risen from modest circumstances to wealth and social position; surely ordinary workmen saw some of their fellows move into the entrepreneurial ranks; surely some of the wealthy lost their gains because of defects of character—but at the same time one could point to the great numbers who remained poor or struggled on for a lifetime as wage earners despite their best efforts; or to the trampling of the virtues of the success ethic by unscrupulous men who discovered other means to wealth; or to the advantages that inheritance and education established for the middle and upper classes. Thus, argument became as important as fact, and when one considers the massed forces of those who contended that the success ethic described reality, one realizes how formidable was the task of those who might disbelieve.

The child discovered through the McGuffey Readers that the success ethic not only underlay American society, but that it was designed by God. Between 1870 and 1890, approximately 60,000,000 copies of the Readers were sold, and in each the message was constant. As the child became a man, interested in the popular fiction of the day, he learned that the virtues that produced success also led his heroes to their greatest victories. The hero triumphed through his fortitude, ingenuity, and trust in his own ability. Whether he was an adventure hero, or a successful suitor, his correct course invariably was the one sanctioned by the established values of middle-class America. Should the reader be more erudite in his interests, he might read the leading economists of the day, and most, even after the work of Richard Ely, Edward James, and other New Economists appeared in the 1880's, stressed the absolute validity of the natural laws of economics. The laissez-faire ideas of Arthur Perry, Amasa Walker, and Lyman Atwater dominated the treatises, textbooks, respectable journals, and lecture halls. Should the citizen seek more concrete comments on how to make sense of the economic order, he would confront a wealth of popular manuals, all of which reinforced the fundamental values of the success ethic. Should the thinking man seek spiritual solace, he would find that the clergy stressed the same virtues, glorified the struggle for success, and offered the opinion that "It is a religious duty to work for the good of this country, and it is not easy to imagine that any one can love God or man and hate America." [4]

Certainly there were men who opposed these views—and they were often men of distinction and humanity—but they were in the minority, and their access to the public was usually limited. The supporters of the social gospel cried out that competition and individual gain contradicted Christ's message and destroyed all hopes for the brotherhood of man. Although the hierarchy of the Catholic Church generally remained conservative, leading Catholic laymen publicized the poor conditions faced by most Catholic workers, and they demanded an improvement in the standard of living through the acceptance of trade unions and the use of social legislation. Richard Ely, John Commons and other younger economists, often influenced by the social gospel, attacked the orthodox laissez-faire theory and argued that social idealism should influence the economic order. Labor leaders claimed the success ethic falsified reality in innumerable ways, that the worker found his condition growing less satisfactory in the midst of a great outpouring of wealth, and that only collective action through the trade union could remedy this situation. Reformers, disunited in their solutions for the evils they saw before them, united around the firm conviction that America had deluded itself into accepting the grossest imperfections as universal values, while the socialists, who characterized American society as exploitative, hypocritical, and immoral, proposed a new morality and a new society based upon the utter denial of the success ethic.

The success ethic had appealed to Americans because it emphasized an equality of opportunity based upon hard work and talent rather than on great amounts of wealth or special education. However, the pattern of economic growth in the last three decades of the nineteenth century reduced the possibility of achieving success through the means suggested by the ethic (Source 4). The extension of the railroad trackage from about 52,000 miles in 1870 to over 166,000 miles in 1890, combined with the creation of integrated railroad systems, made a true national market possible. Large corporations emerged to take

[4] J. L. Spalding, "Are We in Danger of Revolution?" *The Forum*, I (July 1886), 415.

advantage of the more extensive sales opportunities. Compared with older enterprises, these firms required huge amounts of capital for plant and machinery. In the 1860's and 1870's, an investment of $50,000–$100,000 was sufficient for even the most mechanized and complex plants, but by the 1890's, capitalizations of $1,000,000 were not large. In the 1870's, most firms were still small, and they served a rather limited market. By 1900, most of the major industries were dominated by a few large companies that were often vertically integrated so that all phases of the business from the production of raw materials to the sale of the finished product were under a centralized management. Although the greatest period for industrial mergers was the half dozen years following 1897, there was a significant combination of smaller manufacturing units into larger ones during the 1880's and early 1890's. Even where the concentration of an industry into the hands of a few firms was not pronounced, competition among companies in an enlarged market, and under the influence of new technological advances, required larger and larger capital outlays. Thus, the small entrepreneur increasingly faced stiff competition from corporations operating on a regional or national basis.

The small entrepreneur did not disappear from the American economy, but clearly his role in manufacturing diminished. This shift was not sudden or complete. Many small enterprises did persist in the manufacturing areas while new ones proliferated in service and trade areas. The small entrepreneurs increasingly turned to the opportunities offered as middlemen and retailers in an expanding national economy.

Thus, opportunity did not disappear for men of modest means who might seek to enter the business classes from the ranks of labor. However, the breakdown of the traditional link between skilled work and success as an entrepreneur in the same skilled trade; the increasing numbers of unskilled industrial workers, paid at minimal levels and lacking both skill and capital; the severity of the depressions of 1873 and 1893, which dislocated small business as well as the giant concerns —all these taken together with the larger size of business enterprises, the nationalization of markets, and the rapid changes produced by technology and centralized management reduced the likelihood that a workingman could fulfill the terms of the success ethic. Many social critics pointed out that the ethic better fit the small businesses, local markets, and unmechanized production techniques that characterized so much of ante-bellum America than the rapidly changing economy of the last third of the century.

Despite these economic changes, the success ethic did not lose its supporters, and it continued to be a basic element in the American creed. However, to many conservatives, the ethic now became a defense of the status quo instead of a promise of fluidity and change. They realized full well that as long as workers sought success through the traditional means, the possibilities of an attack upon private property and upon great differences in wealth would be nil. As long as the American worker was an incipient capitalist, he would not become a radical. The critics were also present, and their influence increased as America became more thoroughly industrialized, and the cracks in the success formula began to appear more clearly. However, the basic principles of the success ethic did survive, and they continued to constitute the most widely accepted view of the American worker's position in society.

III

In the last third of the nineteenth century, over ten million immigrants entered the United States. Unlike many of the immigrants who arrived before 1860, these newcomers generally became industrial workers; and it soon became obvious that in the mill towns of New England, the coal mines and steel plants of Pennsylvania, and the tenement-filled ghettos of major cities, the immigrant lived in poor, often desperate conditions, isolated from any real contact with native-born Americans, exploited by his fellow countrymen as well as by the Yankees, and seemingly far removed from the success ethic and American values. Could these foreign-born masses fit into the position established by the success ethic for the American worker?

Although Americans were generally prepared to concede that the foreign-born worker might be necessary for the growth of the nation, they usually reacted to the newly arrived immigrant with strong personal antagonism. British immigrants experienced the least prejudice, while the Irish, Chinese—and after 1885—the Southern and Eastern European immigrants, met the strongest hostility. Periodically, this strong prejudice burst the bounds of physical separation and social condemnation and reached the political arena in movements such as the nativists and Know-Nothings of the pre-Civil War period and the restrictionists of the 1880's and 1890's. Strong distaste for the recent immigrants could be found in most elements of society, including the Brahmins of Boston, the racists of the John Fiske-John Burgess type, the upper class directors of the charitable societies, the urban middle class, and the native-born American worker (Sources 5 and 6). Even an established immigrant community could have a distaste for a newly arrived group quite as strong as that found among native born Americans.

In addition to this generalized hostility to the immigrant, many workingmen seemed to regard the newcomers as competitors for jobs. Skilled workers frequently complained that immigrants entered their trades and depressed wage levels. Some labor leaders contended that the newcomer could be organized while others argued that he constituted a threat to trade unionism. Although it has been pointed out that new-comers generally took the poorest jobs and that older immigrant groups moved to better paying positions, this development occurred only gradually, and it primarily affected the second generation. Most first generation immigrants continued to work at unskilled or semi-skilled labor, and they felt the impact of the newcomer most strongly. This led steel companies, for example, to employ a multi-lingual work force composed primarily of newcomers and first generation immigrants. It was hoped that the tensions among these workers would block the growth of unionism and keep labor costs at a minimum. The criticism of the newcomer as an unfair, low wage competitor blended with the prejudice that arose among workers because of differences in nationality, religion, and race (the Negro experienced much of the same hostility as the newcomer from abroad) as well as dissimilar habits and attitudes. The result was a personal distaste for the newcomer equal in intensity to that exhibited by the middle and upper classes of American society (Source 7).

This strong personal dislike for the newly arrived immigrant did not lead to a concerted campaign for restriction until the mid-1880's. As a spokesman for the New York Association for Improving the Condition of the Poor wrote in 1867, after the Association had made a searing indictment of the foreign-born population in New York City:

"Let it not for a moment be imagined that the prominence which has been given to our foreign population is attributable to prejudice or unkindness. . . . The ignorance, debasement and wretchedness of many should excite a more active and earnest concern in their behalf." [5] If the newcomers were as degraded as the Association believed, would such a concern be likely to grow, or would Americans reject them as unfit for the responsibilities imposed by the success ethic?

In the 1880's and 1890's, there was increased discussion of the supposed differences between the older immigrants from Britain, Germany, and Scandinavia, and newcomers from Southern and Eastern Europe. Stress fell on ethnic differences, and much was written about the superiority of the Northern European immigrants. The older immigrants were praised for having assimilated so readily, as well as for their recognizable upward mobility, which testified to the opportunities offered in America. In contrast, the Southern and Eastern Europeans were charged with clannishness and hostility to American ways and values. Furthermore, their poverty was cited as evidence of their inferiority.

Despite this emphasis upon ethnic factors in the final years of the century, American attitudes toward immigrants had been determined, in practice, much more by the economic situation of the newcomers than by their ethnic character. In fact, the undesirable characteristics ascribed to newly arrived immigrants varied little between mid-century and 1900. In part they were stereotypes that owed more to prejudice and social distance than to reality. However, many of these traits were those usually charged to the poor, rather than special characteristics of the foreign-born. Thus the newcomer was often charged with intemperance and ignorance, with a menial mentality and political allegiance to corrupt leaders, and with a pervasive criminality and immorality. To the degree that these conditions did exist, they were just as prevalent among poor native-born Americans.

For example, it mattered little that the Irish were "older" immigrants from Northern Europe. The poverty of most Irish immigrants, their concentration in urban ghettos, plus the hostility that could be generated against Catholics, led to strong prejudice against Irish-

---

[5] New York Association for Improving the Condition of the Poor, *Annual Report*, No. 24 (1867), 44.

Americans. Large numbers of German and Scandinavian immigrants continued to enter the United States during the 1870's and 1880's, but unlike many of their countrymen who had preceded them, these newcomers from Northern Europe became semiskilled or unskilled industrial workers. They shared in the poverty and ghetto life so widespread among Southern and Eastern European immigrants, and it is not surprising that they encountered much of the same prejudice.

On the other hand, the British immigrants who entered the United States in these decades met with a minimum of personal hostility and prejudice. The British immigrant often came with skills that allowed him to move into the skilled trades or even the lower managerial ranks. This permitted these newcomers to adopt American consumption standards more quickly than groups that came with fewer advantages. Thus the mobility exhibited by British immigrants, along with their rapid assimilation, was taken as evidence of their desirability.

It is also interesting to note that the restrictionists of the late 1880's and 1890's turned to the literacy test. They claimed that such a test would exclude Southern and Eastern European ethnic groups in favor of those from Western and Northern Europe. However, we should be aware that such a device also tended to exclude the poorest and least skilled immigrants—whatever their origins. The newcomer who finally entered the United States would be better equipped to compete in the job market and to secure the minimum in income that would encourage a rapid acceptance of American values and quick assimilation.

Keeping these attitudes in mind, one can see the gulf between the negative view toward the newly arrived immigrants and the positive obligations of the success ethic. Americans often ascribed the traits of the newcomer to racial character or the degrading, servile experience of living in the despotic European states. However, the source of the newcomer's inferiority was less important than the result: He was ideologically excluded from American society. The contradiction between American values of equal opportunity and the growth of a large population that seemingly failed to share the necessary qualities was resolved by denying that the immigrants were truly Americans. They lived and worked here; they might be necessary for the growth of the nation's industry—but they were not really part of the nation.

Prejudice and distaste finally banished the newly arrived immigrant into his own world of hard manual labor and grinding poverty, and, at the same time, solved the inconsistency between reality and attitude.

When the immigrant rose to a more middle-class style of life; when he left the ghetto for newer areas of the city, or accumulated savings or property; when his children accepted American values, even if it meant the rejection of their parents' European ways—when, in sum, the foreign-born or second-generation individual had lost the qualities that marked him off as a newcomer and had become more thoroughly Americanized, then could he enter into the American value system, and then would he receive a grudging, if not hospitable, welcome. America was still viewed as a haven for the oppressed, but that notion seemed to be honored more as historical truth than as present reality. One could point to those foreign-born groups who had proved that America was a land of opportunity—including one's own ethnic group, of course—and this could include immigrants of comparatively recent vintage, as long as they had lost the characteristics of poverty and distinctiveness that characterized them upon entry. Thus, the ideological exclusion of the immigrant was not fixed, and should the newcomer surmount his supposed servility and inferiority, the nation stood ready to accept him.

There were those who objected to the idea that the newly arrived immigrant was inferior. They argued that the undesirable qualities of the immigrant were the result of poverty, and were thus remediable through trade unionism (Source 8). The same solution was offered for the problems that beset native-born workers. Jane Addams, and the other leaders of the settlement house movement of the 1890's, insisted that the newcomer suffered from an environmental deprivation *in* America, not from any basic inferiority. The settlements were designed to help him overcome the disadvantages of poverty and segregation in ethnic ghettos. Others defended the need for foreign-born labor without necessarily challenging the fundamental attitudes toward the newcomer. Spokesmen for the immigrants denied the charge of inferiority and pointed to the rapid rise of their groups into middle-class society.

However, the strong prejudice against the more recent immigrants remained and helped increase the negative attitude toward manual labor. As the newcomer took the lowest paying, most onerous forms of work, these manual occupations began to lose their traditional dignity as the starting point and training ground for the American worker who expected to move upward to eventual self-employment. Instead they took on the low esteem given to those who now filled them. Unskilled manual labor became increasingly the province of each new wave of immigrants, and the vicious circle was soon established of men looked down upon because of their work and work looked down upon because of the men who performed it.

The newcomer faced a rough road should he seek a better life. Aside from prejudice, the obvious handicap of a hesitant command of English, and an incomplete knowledge of American customs and manners, the new immigrant often lacked a skilled trade, and thus he went into the lowest-paying occupations. This made it necessary for him to live in the poorest quarters of the cities, frequently in ethnic ghettos (Source 9). In many cases, low wages forced his wife and children to work, and should the newcomer have close relatives in Europe, part of his scanty wages might be sent abroad. The hard work, crowded slums, and disdain of the native-born Americans might stimulate an intense desire to move upward, but it might also produce hopelessness and acceptance.

Investigations into the mobility of immigrants reveal sharp differences, and they are not conclusive. However, a cautious overall judgment does seem justified. The immigrant found mobility to be difficult, and limited, and the majority of the first generation advanced only slightly. Often this improvement was secured through the accumulation of some savings which made it possible to move to newer residential areas and/or purchase a house. It was thus mobility through a careful husbanding of resources and the acquisition of some small amount of property rather than a move to a better-paying, higher-status occupation. The conditions of life for the immigrant, though often poor by American standards, usually rivalled or exceeded the economic situation in Europe, and increased religious and political freedom compensated many for the hardships they faced on this side of the Atlantic. Many immigrants achieved little occupational or property mobility, and it would seem that at any one time, only a minority of the first generation was making any real advance. There were widespread variations, however, because of the different values brought to America by each ethnic group, the distinctive conditions encountered in various areas of the United States, and basic institutional factors, such as the rate of growth of the economy and the rapidity with which industrialization created higher-status jobs.

The second generation usually made much more significant advances in occupational mobility, with many persons moving into skilled labor, or into white collar positions and the lower grades of the supervisory ranks. Once again the movement was not general, and it was affected by ethnic, institutional, and personal factors. We might characterize this mobility as significant but not universal. It was clearly a gain for the second-generation individual, and it usually secured him enough acceptance to break down the most extreme forms of prejudice and the impression of inherent inferiority. However, this second-generation mobility was slow enough so that these persons felt the competition of the newest immigrants quite keenly, and a sharp antipathy often developed from this rivalry.

Conclusions concerning mobility cannot be firm for either the immigrant or the native-born worker. Differences in the rate and type of mobility must be recognized. Individual factors could lead some families to run counter to the general trend for their ethnic group or for American workers as a whole. Nineteenth-century studies of workingmen's budgets and home conditions graphically show how men, who would have been classified together in a quantitative sense, were far apart in a qualitative sense. Ambition and skill were only part of the difference; luck, avoidance of illness, and size of family were other important variables (Source 10).

The criteria used to measure mobility are not always constant, and thus some investigators describe intragenerational mobility while others examine intergenerational changes. The results obtained are different, as noted earlier. We may also consider mobility only in occupational terms, or accept property acquisition and changes of neighborhood as evidence of an advance. Once again, the choice of the yardstick affects the results in a significant fashion. Attempts to examine specific families—rather than general figures drawn from census reports and state tabulations about savings, occupational distribution, and home ownership—promise a surer base for judgment; but such a study runs into the basic problem of transience. The less successful workers moved frequently, and thus local records lost track of them. The results will reflect the conditions that prevailed among the more stable and probably more successful families.[6] Thus, definite judgments about mobility are difficult because of methodological problems, inadequate sources, and variations of a significant order.

Of course, the newcomer who arrived in the late nineteenth century did not think in terms of defining the character of mobility and measuring its extent. He faced a basic American success ethic, a more specific set of prejudices against himself, and the realities of his economic and social situation. From this he would fashion his own attitudes concerning the promise offered by America.

Writers in the late nineteenth century frequently charged the immigrant with the un-American attitude of class consciousness. In actuality, the foreign-born accepted basic American values centering around mobility and an open society. Immigrants came to America from a variety of situations. Some came because economic changes in Europe threatened to convert them from skilled workers to factory laborers, or from tenant farmers to agricultural laborers; some came because there seemed little economic opportunity of any sort at home, and work, even at low wages, meant much in comparison with continuous underemployment; some came because letters from relatives and friends stressed the opportunity to make one's own way to a better life, while others responded to the advertisements of the shipping companies which also extolled the openness of American society. Men who were truly class-conscious or fatalistic tended to remain in Europe, and it was the adventurous, the ambitious, and the dissatisfied who broke the old ties and embarked on the uncertain road. Men who faced religious and political discrimination also sought passage across the Atlantic, but it would seem that the opportunity to enter a mobile society and advance to a living standard unattainable in Europe was the strongest attraction for the immigrant.

Many immigrants failed to achieve significant occupational mobility, although a larger group did gain some measure of status from

---

[6] For an excellent discussion of this point and the many problems involved in studying mobility, see Stephan Thernstrom, *Poverty and Progress: Social Mobility in a Nineteenth-Century City* (Cambridge, Mass.: Harvard University Press, 1964).

the acquisition of property. America could produce the same type of fixed and arduous existence they had left behind in Europe. Immigrants who failed to advance might become fatalistic and abandon their hope for upward mobility, or they might adopt the class consciousness they had tried to discard when crossing the ocean. Radicalism could easily attract such men, for they had been doubly cheated: if neither European nor American society offered a proper life to the working-man, then a radical transformation would seem to be needed.

In the three decades following 1880, large numbers of immigrants returned to their native countries, and the circumstances of this massive repatriation, which reached as much as one-third of the total of incoming persons, reveal once again the attraction of success for the foreign-born. Those who returned home were not the very rich who had succeeded in America, but neither were they the poor, coming to their native land in failure; instead the greatest bulk of the Italian, Greek, and Norwegian immigrants who left America had accumulated a modest amount of savings and believed that the possibilities for the successful use of this money were greater in Europe than in the United States. They returned home to achieve an upward mobility that America had promised, but which seemed elusive or far-distant to a resident of the ghettos. Often a relatively small amount of money would go far in the poorer areas of Europe toward providing the capital for a farm or small business. Some repatriates failed to make a go of it in their native lands and returned ultimately to the United States. Thus, the immigrant who returned to Europe might be more resolutely pursuing upward mobility than those who remained in America and slid into a fatalistic acceptance of poverty. It is thus all the more interesting that the critics of immigration often attacked these "birds of passage" for their exploitation of the American welcome and for their disregard of American values. In fact, they were most resolute believers in the im-portance of being successful.

American trade unionists became increasingly hostile to massive European immigration in the 1880's and 1890's. They argued that the newly arrived worker undercut established American wage scales, thus lowering the standard of living and increasing unemployment among those already here. Moreover, the newcomer sabotaged efforts at trade union action through his refusal to join with his fellow workmen. It is true that many immigrants did not join trade unions, but many did, and the reasons why the foreign-born joined or failed to join are most instructive.

It must first be realized that those immigrants who had been in America for some years, and had acquired a skilled trade, did join the trade unions in considerable numbers. The Illinois Bureau of Labor Statistics reported in 1886 that only twenty-one per cent of the trade unionists in the state had been born in America. The Bureau concluded that the high proportion of foreign-born workers in trade unions resulted from the fact that

> . . . the foreign workman has the traditions of many generations, and the walls of caste to restrain him within certain limits as to his occupation; he has no possibilities beyond a given sphere, and is trained and developed within it. Thus environed, his career and ambitions lie in the paths his fathers trod, and his associations with his fellow craftsmen make the trade-union his natural and necessary place. Transported to this country he brings his feeling for the union and his class associations with him as habit.
>
> But the American mechanic's boy is born to no condition in life from which he may not rise, or hope to rise, or which at least he may not abandon for better or worse.[7]

The Bureau accepted the belief that foreign-born workers were strongly class conscious in comparison with the American mechanic. However, the great majority of the foreign-born skilled workmen remained outside the labor movement just as native-born craftsmen did. Moreover, the longer the immigrant lived in the United States, the more likely he was to adopt American values. As will become clear later in our discussion, membership in a trade union did not necessarily mean the abandonment of the success ethic, and this was as true for native-born as for foreign-born workingmen. Thus, the widespread belief in the distinctive behavior of the immigrant who joined trade unions was hardly justified.

In contrast to the established immigrants, the newly arrived did not readily enter organized labor. Newcomers were often unskilled and easily replaced. For those newcomers who planned to return home after accumulating some capital, strikes were a disaster, for they stopped all work. These men thought in terms of work—at almost any wage, and

[7] Illinois Bureau of Labor Statistics, *Biennial Report*, No. 4 (1886), 228.

under any circumstances—so long as they could save something toward the return home. Many of these newcomers were unmarried, while others had left wives and children behind in Europe. Accordingly, they cared less about improving American working conditions than earning an immediate wage.

Since the newly arrived immigrant was generally unskilled, the trade unions often considered him as a possible threat and as impossible to organize. However, it should be stressed that native-born workers who were unskilled similarly failed to join unions, and the debate is still quite vital as to whether this gap in organized labor's ranks was the product of conservatism and narrow self-interest on the part of the craft unions, or the result of the impossible task of organizing unskilled labor in the hostile, anti-union climate of the late nineteenth and early twentieth centuries. Finally, one must note the prejudice against immigrants, particularly those who had arrived most recently. In sum, it would seem that the newly arrived immigrant often had little interest in the union because it did not serve his objectives, or because he was particularly liable to pressure from his employer. However, for those who might have joined organized labor, the unions often did not exist, and the prejudice within those that did was hardly an attraction.

Although the European immigrant seemed to share the American emphasis upon upward mobility, he saw more quickly that the terms of the conventional success ethic were rapidly losing touch with reality, and he was able to establish standards of success that better met his capabilities. The native-born worker responded more slowly, but eventually he also adjusted the success ethic to the reality of an industrial society.

British immigrants often achieved occupational mobility in America, yet few became entrepreneurs in comparison with the large number who advanced to positions as foremen, superintendents, and inspectors in mills and mines. This type of occupational mobility was more realistic a possibility than entrance into the business classes. Native-born skilled workers also placed increasing emphasis upon movement to a supervisory position rather than the goals of the success ethic— testimony to the attractiveness of the more realistic alternatives.

Many Eastern European immigrants from peasant origins valued home ownership as a mark of status and success. They had no tradition of entrepreneurial activity in their native lands, and the difficulty of accumulating significant amounts of capital made entrance into the American business world most difficult. Many of these immigrants lacked a craft, and only a minority were able to achieve even the modest rise in the occupational scale from unskilled to skilled labor. Thus, the substitution of mobility through home ownership met their needs in this nation, and it conformed to the traditional interest in real property that they had brought with them from Europe.

Newcomers from Greece and newly arrived Jews from Eastern Europe were more familiar with entrepreneurial skills, which they prized more highly. Yet the newcomer who sought to become an employer found that prejudice, lack of capital, and a poor command of American manners often blocked his way; and thus many of those who set up a small business served the immigrant community from which they came. These businessmen discovered that they did not gain the respect from the native-born American that normally might have been expected.

Originally the American success ethic did not stress education as a prerequisite for upward mobility. The traditional virtues were much more important to an equalitarian approach since education was the privilege of the few, and the skills required of the successful entrepreneur were as often learned on the job as in the schoolroom. However, the increasing complexity of an industrial society, and the greater availability of free public schools in the decades after the Civil War, placed a new importance upon formal education. Although it often has been argued that education offered mobility to the poor, both native and foreign-born workingmen frequently placed a much higher value on child labor. Economic need might demand child labor, and for some immigrants the concept of the extended family, based on labor by many related persons, was more important than the possible effects of education upon the future occupational mobility of the children. In fact, property mobility for the first generation might be possible only at the expense of the children's education. Thus, older attitudes that did not value formal education and the harsh realities that demanded extra earning power in the present led many parents to ignore the increasing emphasis on a good education in favor of the increase in income made possible by evasion of the child labor laws or the withdrawal of the child from school as soon as possible. This development serves to illustrate still further the complicated relationship between the goals set by American society for its workingmen and their actual response.

IV

Although the American success ethic focused on the individual's progress, it also included the assumption that society as a whole prospered from the free operation of competition and personal effort. The great increase in wealth produced by the rapid industrialization of the nation and the creation of a true national market were linked by many to the operation of free enterprise capitalism. The success ethic encouraged innovation and progress, and it was the best method of distributing wealth. However, labor leaders and reformers argued that the unparalleled increase in national wealth was being distributed so unequally that the rich only grew richer while the workingmen grew poorer. The discussion included more than material factors, ranging over matters of status and expectations as well.

Carroll Wright, the former chief of the Massachusetts Bureau of Labor Statistics, and, in 1897, the United States Commissioner of Labor, defended the proposition that the American economy benefitted all. Wright did not deny the unequal distribution of wealth, nor did he insist upon the absolute sufficiency of wages; instead Wright argued for the relative increase of all incomes, including those of the workmen. Drawing on his background as a statistician, he tried to prove that the rich were growing richer but so were the poor. Moreover, "there never was a time . . . when the rich did so much for society and for the poor as they are doing at the present time." [8] This relative improvement of the worker's lot was quite aside from exceptional individual effort within the success ethic. Andrew Carnegie wrote in the same vein, and conservatives generally accepted a relative gain for all and the rapid advance of the deserving individual.

The conservative position certainly dominated the popular press and the statements by public officials, but dissent from these arguments was continuous. One line of criticism acknowledged that a few

---

[8] Carroll Wright, "Are the Rich Growing Richer and the Poor Poorer?" *Atlantic Monthly,* LXXX (September 1897), 308.

men could rise from the laboring classes, but concluded "that in spite of the hard work of workingmen from their early youth to advanced age, they are steadily getting poorer, while the capitalistic class increases their wealth and social and political power." [9] Thus the undeniable increase in the total wealth of the country meant little to the worker. In commenting on the growth of wealth in Massachusetts, one reformer vividly put the case:

> But it is beginning to be apparent that she [Massachusetts] is increasing her property at the expense of her people; that the rich are growing richer and the poor poorer; that increase of culture and increase of ignorance are going on side by side; and thus that while her money is accumulating, her men are deteriorating.[10]

A second line of criticism did not seek to deny the improvement in the standard of living of many workingmen, which had accompanied industrial growth. However, as John Commons pointed out:

> Men do not compare themselves with their ancestors, but with their contemporaries. You cannot appease a restless workman by telling him how much better off he is than his simian progenitor. What he feels is his dependence on his fellowman, who is growing richer every day upon the fruits of his poorly paid toil.[11]

The constant discontent expressed by labor leaders appeared to Josiah Strong to be the result of inadequate gains, not a total lack of progress. The influential advocate of the eight-hour day, Ira Steward, had argued that increasing wants produced a higher standard of living. Strong believed this had already happened by 1893, and thus American workers demanded an equitable share in the nation's progress (Source 11).

Most of the trade union leaders agreed with Strong: more and more meant an equitable sharing of the increasing wealth, not the meager gains that overflowed from a bursting economy. By and large,

---

[9] *The Hammer,* V (November 1886), 1.
[10] *Equity,* I (April 1874), 3.
[11] John Commons, *Social Reform and the Church* (New York: Thomas Y. Crowell & Co., 1894), p. 7. Commons was just beginning his career at this point. He later became a leading advocate of labor legislation, and one of the greatest of American labor historians.

American workers also thought in relative terms. As their expectations rose, they found that their real earnings were inadequate, even though these earnings were often absolutely higher than in past decades. The premium placed on achieving the middle class often left the worker with an increasing gap between rising wages and climbing expectations.

The critics also emphasized the false hopes of mobility offered by the success ethic. Henry George focused on the changes that industrialization had made in the conditions that spawned the success ethic. He compared these changes with a train departing from a station:

> When a railway train is slowly moving off, a single step may put one on it. But in a few minutes those who have not taken that step may run themselves out of breath in the hopeless endeavour to overtake the train. . . . So it is absurd to think that opportunities open when steam and machinery were beginning their concentrating work will remain open.[12]

Many observers stressed that the concentration of industry into huge corporations or trusts effectively blocked the man who would enter from below. Complicated techniques of production, and the large amounts of capital needed to begin most enterprises, similarly dashed the hopes of those who would seek to become entrepreneurs. The success ethic was viewed as an anachronism, but a dangerous one, since it blinded workingmen to the reality of their situation.

Most American workingmen did not quarrel with capitalism, but with their exclusion from full participation in it. Thus, it is not surprising that so many observers—be they conservatives or radicals, employers or labor leaders, spokesmen for the success ethic or reformers who denied its relevance—could agree on the commitment of the American worker to the general principles of the success ideology, including an absence of class consciousness and fixed class lines, and a strong desire for upward mobility of some sort (Source 12).

Conservatives noted with satisfaction that "Property is too widely diffused here for property to be abolished. You cannot here make the

---

[12] Henry George, *Social Problems* (Chicago: Belford, Clarke and Co., 1883), pp. 66–67.

socialistic spark fire the powder of the workingman's discontent." [13] It was only one step more to contend that any support for socialism in the United States must be among foreign-born workers, and that the socialists' critique had no application to American conditions. The socialists conceded that "notwithstanding the existence of so much overwhelming evidence of the impossibility for *all* to become rich by honest industry and economy and for but *few* to become rich even by unfair means, the great mass of our people suppose that all with industry and economy may at last become independent." [14] A socialist writer chastized those workers who "quietly pursue their own self-culture and train their offspring to enter and swell the large class of unproductive 'middlemen' that they at the very least may escape the degrading influences of productive labor." [15]

Many labor leaders would have accepted the conclusions of a writer in *John Swinton's Paper* when he wrote "that the majority of men (capitalists, employers, foremen and workmen themselves) are actuated by about the same ideas and principles—the lust of lucre and power." [16] Moreover, it is interesting to observe that labor newspapers printed excerpts from success manuals even in the midst of the depression of the 1870's. Labor unions had to battle against the idea that the merit and skill of the individual worker would earn its full reward; instead they contended that only organization could guarantee that the employer would meet his responsibilities to his employees (Source 13).

Even though the basic principles of the success ideology were generally accepted by American workers, there seems to have been less and less attention paid by even skilled, native-born workmen to the literal provisions of the success ethic, with its emphasis on an advance into the entrepreneurial class. Instead, some workingmen were attracted to cooperative schemes for establishing businesses that could be owned by the employees, while others joined trade unions which sought to impose a collective minimum for all members. However, most workers

---

[13] Joseph Cook, "Self Help, State Help and Church Help for Workingmen," *Labor, Its Rights and Wrongs* (Washington, D.C.: Labor Publishing Co., 1886), p. 110.
[14] "Can All Get Rich?" *The Socialist* (July 29, 1876), 2.
[15] E. King, "Labor and Degradation," *The Toiler*, I (September 26, 1874), 1.
[16] *John Swinton's Paper* (February 8, 1885), 1.

adopted neither of these approaches, but instead developed the same type of property and consumption standards of mobility that we observed among immigrant groups.

Native-born workers increasingly realized that mobility into the entrepreneurial class was unlikely, especially in industries or trades dominated by large companies selling to larger and larger markets (Source 14). Thus, workers substituted other criteria for the occupational standard. Promotion to supervisory ranks became an extremely important goal for skilled workers in industries such as railroads or steel. The journals of the railroad brotherhoods frequently extolled the dignity of the worker and his ability to advance to a still higher position, even superintendent of a line (Source 15). It is obvious that membership in a union had not ended the desire for individual advancement. But this sort of mobility was more in touch with reality than the pathway proposed in the success ethic.

Moreover, the desire for promotion slaked the bitterness and jealousy that might have been produced by the high salaries paid to management. Thus, the editor of the *Locomotive Firemen's Magazine* contended that the employees of the New York Central Railroad did not begrudge President Chauncey Depew his annual salary of $75,000. "It is true that some poor fellow working the whole day, and every day, for a few cents and struggling to support his family, might wish that he too was more fortunate. . . ."[17]

Skilled workers also insisted on the consumption levels of the middle class even though this badly strained their budgets. Foreign visitors commented on the similarity in home furnishings and clothing between skilled workers and members of the middle class. While the worker protested about his dignity, when compared to the white collar employee, he aspired to the items prized by those very same elements of the nonmanual work force. In a period when installment credit was not yet sanctioned as a means of stretching the worker's income, mobility through the achievement of a middle-class consumption level was even more difficult, and this was certainly one major element in the discontent about wages noted so frequently in the 1880's and 1890's.

[17] W. S. Carter, "The Employees," *Locomotive Firemen's Magazine*, XXIV (April 1898), 387.

Workingmen also gave thought to earning a "competence," i.e., savings sufficient to provide for their old age, and ample enough to serve as a source for investment in property or stock. The competence became an important measure of having "gotten on in the world." However, testimony by workers indicated that even skilled craftsmen had difficulty saving any sizable amount of money. Many fell into debt. Some workers did acquire property or savings, and there was much discussion over the actual extent of the deposits by workingmen in savings banks. It would seem that these deposits were considerable in total, but small per capita. The competence was a thoroughly middle-class device, one carrying respect, and certainly a mark of status. However, it would seem that few workers could acquire much money without occupational mobility. Thus, many workingmen placed emphasis on the more attainable goal of acquiring their own house and lot. The native-born worker thus joined the immigrant in using home ownership as a measure of mobility.

Many conservatives regarded this as a healthy situation, since property ownership helped check radical sentiments. It also reduced the worker's geographical mobility, making it easier to secure employees at the desired wages. It is thus not surprising that those workers who lacked secure jobs or badly-needed skills often refused to consider home ownership for fear it would strip away their physical mobility—one of the few protections they had against an imperious employer or unemployment. Stephan Thernstrom, in his study of Newburyport, Massachusetts, found a tremendous turnover in the work force; home ownership was of most importance among the more stable, usually more skilled or better-established workers. Of course, home ownership did not lift the individual from the ranks of the manual workers, but it was a means of acquiring a sense of upward movement.

The reports of state bureaus of labor statistics also stressed home ownership as a major element in determining the standard of living of the worker. Homes often sold for as little as $600, and thus better-paid workmen, and the more frugal among the unskilled, could acquire a small house and lot. In small towns, where the labor force was more stable, home ownership took on great importance; but even in large cities workers sought homes in newer areas of the municipality. Thus, most workingmen did not adopt the collective approach of the trade union or the millennialism of the radical; instead they attempted to adjust to the conditions around them while still retaining a belief in upward individual mobility, which was now defined in terms more suitable to their actual situation.

A major source of concern for all American workingmen, and especially the skilled, was the increasing application of capital to the productive process through the development and use of machinery. Industrialization was based upon the use of machines in factories, with the consequent centralization of the labor supply, the increase in the volume of production, and the reduction of cost. The skilled worker faced one of the initial waves of change that flowed from industrialization (Source 16). Primarily native-born, or of long-term residence, the skilled worker was most likely to conform to the dictates of the success ethic, though the great majority failed to do so. The increasing use of machinery made the small shop, based upon the quality of craftsmanship, less viable, and instead the entrepreneur required large amounts of capital to purchase new equipment and to build factories. The effect on the skilled worker was double-barrelled. He often saw his part in production fractured into a number of mechanical processes easily handled by unskilled workmen. This could mean a decline in wages, as it did for skilled workers in the steel industry. Even where wages did not decline significantly, there might still occur the less calculable but most important loss in social status. Skilled workmen were now barred from entrance into the entrepreneurial class because the new enterprises depended less on the skill and knowledge acquired by a craftsman than on the capital and managerial talent available to the promoter.

A committee appointed by the American Social Science Association in 1878 concluded that machinery had

> . . . broken up and destroyed our whole system of individual and independent action in production and manufacture, where any man who possessed a trade by his own hands could at once make that trade his support and means of advancement, free of control by any other man, and has compelled all working men and women to a system of communal work where, in hundreds and thousands they are forced to labor with no other interest in the work than is granted to them in wages paid for so much toil; with no voice, no right, no interest in the product of their hands and brains, but subject to the

uncontrolled interest and caprice of those who, too often, know no other motive than that of avarice.[18]

Not only did laborsaving machinery discourage mobility, but it created a sense of dependence among the workers. The success ethic had called for independent effort, and the businessman was so highly prized, in part, because he continued the tradition of independence that characterized the Jeffersonian yeoman or the frontiersman of popular imagination. The skilled worker now found his upward advance stymied, and mechanization made him increasingly dependent on others for his very livelihood.

To those reformers who demanded the end of the wage system itself, it was obvious that "Wherever one man's bread is controlled by another, the man whose bread is controlled by another, *he is that other man's slave.*" [19] They regarded the growth of organized labor as evidence of the increasing dependence of the worker. Originally labor leaders were also unhappy when confronted with the loss of the worker's traditional independence. However, organized labor eventually accepted dependence as an inevitable result of industrialization, and the trade unions were determined to protect the worker from its worst effects.

Those who attacked the deleterious effects of the machine did not argue that mechanization produced no benefits. They admitted the reduction of cost for many items, and the increased availability of goods. However, it was charged that the skilled worker lost more directly, as an individual workman affected by the machine in the productive portion of the economy, than he gained indirectly as a consumer. Critics of mechanization asserted that the greatest part of the efficiency and cost-saving effect of the machinery was taken by the employer as profit, while the worker often found his skill made useless and his very job made more insecure. Although unemployment was not a result of mechanization alone, it was argued that machines so increased the supply of goods that the market needs were met in fewer working days than in the past. Of course, more workers were now employed, but to many skilled workmen, the result of mechanization seemed to be less work, not more. Leading reformers believed that production was

---

[18] W. Godwin Moody, *Our Labor Difficulties: The Cause and the Way Out* (Boston: A. Williams and Co., 1878), p. 80.
[19] *Equity*, I (July 1874), 27.

outstripping demand, and unless the hours of work were cut, without a reduction of pay, and unless the worker had more leisure time in which to develop new needs, which would generate the steam for higher wages, the economy would be drowned in a flood of goods without markets. The result for the worker could only be persistent and regular periods of unemployment.

Whether the skilled worker believed that he would move upward to the entrepreneurial class, or whether he accepted a fixed position, the threat of the unskilled workman was a real one. Constant improvements in manufacturing techniques imperiled the basis of the skilled worker's distinction; the breakdown of the old apprenticeship system threatened to flood the job market with craftsmen, poorly trained, perhaps, but still able to compete with those already at work; and the appearance of foreign-born craftsmen added still another source of skilled labor. This last factor led many workers to support immigration restriction, even before labor unions took a position on the question. The first two developments created a gulf between skilled and unskilled labor, for the craftsmen viewed the unskilled as competitors and not as comrades—as allies of the employer and not as members of a united producing class. Many skilled workers undoubtedly agreed with the editor of a building trades journal when he wrote that the "mechanic and unskilled labor have no interests in common, and whatever is gained by unskilled labor is at the expense of skilled labor" (Source 17).

Skilled workers might turn to the trade union in an effort to gain some measure of job control; but only in a comparatively few trades, and even there, only in certain areas, was the union able to gain control of the job through the closed shop, apprenticeship requirements, and work rules. One of the issues that distinguished the Knights of Labor from the trade unions and the A.F.L. was the Knights' insistence upon the orgnization of unskilled workers and upon the community of interest between craftsmen and laborers. Unless unskilled labor was organized, and unless its wages and working conditions were adequate, men would continuously attempt to move into the ranks of the skilled in search of a better life. The greatest protection for the craftsman was the satisfaction of the common laborer with his position, and this could only be accomplished if the one big union—the Knights of Labor— united the entire work force in an effort to improve conditions for all ranks of workingmen. Terence V. Powderly was particularly bitter towards the skilled worker, and he linked the formation of the Knights directly to their refusal to see beyond their narrow trade interests to the welfare of all workmen.

Thus the skilled workingman strove to maintain his position amid changes that made older attitudes and actions obsolete. Some reactions indicated a desire to retain the old, some acknowledged and accepted the new. In material terms, the conditions of skilled workers as a group improved somewhat as real wages rose between 1865 and 1890; but this rise was extremely slow to 1880, and there is much testimony that the depression of the 1870's caused widespread distress. In terms of status, the worker found that older attitudes no longer fit, and he had to seek new ways to retain the traditional American belief in mobility, a decent standard of living, and the right of all men to a certain dignity. The success ethic could still be stated by authors and journalists in its pristine form, and the middle class might still believe in it; but the skilled worker developed his own variations of the ethic, molding it to fit reality, while he retained the basic conservatism upon which the ethic rested. These accommodations sometimes resembled those made by the immigrants, and even when they varied, both groups of workingmen did share one basic characteristic: a desire to remake and reorder their lives and attitudes to fit a fundamental Americanism rather than to remake America to fit the most realistic view of their immediate needs.

V

Programs of social action are based on some perception of what the fundamental structure of society is, what it permits, and what is likely to occur in the future. Trade union leaders, and reformers interested in the condition of the workingman, had to come to some conclusions about the position of the worker. They had to consider the possibilities for social mobility through the conventional success ethic, or through a society modified to make this ethic more effective, as well as the changes industrialization promised for the nation.

Two sharply different programs emerged from this analysis. The first was based upon the belief that the advance of the worker into the entrepreneurial ranks must be preserved and encouraged, and that labor and reform organizations must operate to free society from conditions that would impede this mobility. Cooperatives, monetary reform, the reduction of hours, and political action were means of preserving the mobility supposedly present in antebellum years. American workers had to avoid the permanent, wage-earning working class associated with Great Britain and other less favored nations of Europe.

The second group argued that industrialization was an irresistible force. It would inevitably destroy the assumptions of the success ethic by creating a fixed working class. Thus one must accept the reality and work out trade union procedures and reform programs that would improve the condition of the worker as a worker. Social mobility would have to be defined in terms of a collective improvement in the standard of living rather than the conversion of the worker into an employer. Both positions had continuous support during the period, 1865–1896, but, as we will observe, the struggle between the two views was most crucial in the 1860's and 1870's. By the 1880's, the tide of industrialization began to make it clearer and clearer that the old success ethic could not be preserved, and although the supporters of individual mobility were still numerous, and often quite influential, the proponents of a labor and reform program that accepted the fixed position of the worker took command. The decade of the 1890's only strengthened this development.

The 1860's and early 1870's clearly reveal the conflict within organized labor over objectives and programs. Trade unionists disagreed on whether the labor union was the ultimate form of organization for the worker or a temporary institution that sought the end of the wage system and thus of its own need for being. Many unionists still refused to accept a strict division between the employer and employee, and thus the International Typographical Union permitted "such employers as may be practical printers" to join.[20] The Carpenters' and Joiners' National Union limited membership to journeymen but permitted "Those members who have been initiated as journeymen and afterwards become employers [to] retain their membership by complying with the laws, and by employing Union Carpenters in preference to others."[21] In contrast, the Cigar Makers' International Union deter-

---

[20] International Typographical Union, *Proceedings* (1865), p. 72.
[21] Carpenters' and Joiners' National Union, *Proceedings* (1866), p. 79.

mined that local unions should be composed of "practical journeymen cigar makers," which was then further defined as a "cigar maker who is employed to be paid by the thousand." [22] Obviously this careful statement was made to exclude employers. By 1890, this confusion over the distinct composition of a trade union had ended, and employers, no matter how small, were excluded. This development was part of the acceptance by trade unionists of the relative fixity of a workingman's position in American society.

The leaders of organized labor also differed in their response to the basic American contention that a mutuality of interest bound the workingman and his employer together in a relationship equally advantageous to both parties. One group agreed with John Oberly, President of the International Typographical Union, that "an infringement of the rights of capital is a blow to the interests of labor, since . . . capital is the goose which lays the golden egg that enriches labor" [23] (Source 18). However, they also agreed that capital did not always have due regard for the rights and interests of the worker, and when this occurred—all too frequently—the trade union had the duty to force capital to act in the spirit of mutuality of interest and treat the employee justly. This group had no fundamental quarrel with the success ethic, capitalism, or mutuality of interest, but it did not see them operating automatically to benefit the laboring man. The union would see to their proper functioning.

The second and largest group of labor leaders, including Samuel Gompers and William Sylvis, openly denied mutuality of interest. Perhaps Sylvis stated this position as clearly in 1864 as the leaders of the A.F.L. were to do two or three decades later:

> If workingmen and capitalists are equal co-partners, composing one vast firm by which the industry of the world is carried on and controlled, why do they not share equally in the profits? Why does capital take to itself the whole loaf, while labor is left to gather up the crumbs? Why does capital roll in luxury and wealth while labor is left to eke out a miserable existence in poverty and want? Are these the evidences of an identity of interest, of mutual relations, of equal partnership? No, sir. On the contrary they are evidences of an an-

[22] Cigar Makers' International Union, *Proceedings* (1867), p. 49.
[23] International Typographical Union, *Proceedings* (1867), p. 4.

tagonism. . . . On the one side employers are interested, because of profit, to keep down the price of labor; while on the other side, the employees are justified, on account of self-interest, to keep up wages. Thus labor and capital are antagonistic.[24]

The leaders of the A.F.L. agreed, and they concluded that workers had to organize and bargain collectively with the employer. Through their united strength, workingmen would continuously increase their wages, shorten their hours, and generally improve their conditions of labor. Identity of interest merely confused the worker and made it certain that his welfare would be subordinated to the needs of the employer.

Sylvis also argued that unions were needed to protect the laboring man. However, unlike the leaders of the A.F.L. and many unionists in his own day, he did not believe that trade unions could permanently improve the condition of the worker. Only the abolition of the distinction between capital and labor—in fact, the elimination of the worker as a wage earner dependent on another's capital for sustenance—could accomplish that. Sylvis proposed producers' cooperatives, which would unite capital and labor in the same persons, and thus eliminate the antagonisms and deprivations of a wage system.

Obviously these arguments directly contravened the mutuality of interest that loomed so large in the success ethic. Proponents of that ethic thus attacked the views of Sylvis and the leaders of the A.F.L. almost as sharply as they condemned the class-conscious, class conflict views of the socialists. Gompers, Sylvis, and many other leaders of American trade unions, shared much of the socialists' contempt for the claims of a mutuality of interest. However, they rejected the contention that the capitalist system itself had to be scrapped. Instead, Gompers argued that workers must share more fully in the proceeds of capitalism, and Sylvis hoped that workers would become capitalists. Although their efforts were continuous, the socialists were unable to convert the supporters of either approach.

The national leadership of the Knights of Labor opposed the idea of a conflict of interest between employer and employee. This marked off the Knights from the national trade unions of the 1880's. The leaders of the Knights believed in a unity of interest among men of approxi-

[24] James Sylvis, ed., *The Life, Speeches, Labors and Essays of William Sylvis* (Philadelphia: Claxton, Remsen and Haffelfinger, 1872), pp. 100–102.

mately equal social class, regardless of whether they were workers or employers. Therefore, employers and the self-employed were permitted to join. Skilled craftsmen and unskilled industrial workers, farmers and small shopkeepers, small businessmen in close touch with their employees, and the self-employed—all had more in common with each other than with the bankers and great capitalists who constituted the real enemy.

In the 1880's, the Knights of Labor was weakened by an internal tug of war among the leadership, who opposed strikes, hoped for producers' cooperatives that would convert the worker into an employer, and envisaged the eventual end of the wage system; the trade union elements, that acted much like the trade unions that joined the A.F.L.; and the unskilled and semi-skilled, who poured into the organization in 1884 and 1885 in response to the vague feeling that the Knights could win concessions for their immediate grievances.

The Illinois Bureau of Labor Statistics noted that the Knights had a higher percentage of native-born persons than the trade unions. Its explanation focused on the broader purposes of the Knights, especially the emphasis on "certain measures of public policy," in contrast to the narrower interests of the craft unions. The Knights attracted many diverse elements, but the leadership represented the most basic one: a desire for reform of the capitalist system in line with the success ethic's emphasis on upward mobility and mutuality of interest.

The attempt to retain a common interest between the worker and those whom he hoped to join in the middle class contributed to the widespread emphasis on the trust and the financier as the villains of the piece. There seems to be a strong bond between these attacks on great wealth and economic power, and the commitment to a continuation of the mobility of the worker into the entrepreneurial ranks. As the trade unions in the A.F.L. gave up their commitment to upward mobility for the worker as an individual, and shifted to the improvement of the workingmen's lot through collective action, hostility toward the trust declined. Gompers increasingly looked on the growth of a relatively few big corporations in the major industries as inevitable, and he did not regard this as antagonistic to organized labor's interests. The trade agreement and collective bargaining could be acceptable to the large corporation that controlled its industry, maintained a stable market and pricing system, and easily passed on increased wage costs to the consumer. Large or small, companies that faced sharp competition calculated costs closely, since wage increases were more likely to be absorbed by the concern itself.

After 1900, Gompers and other leaders of the A.F.L. joined the National Civil Federation, an organization sponsored by business leaders, such as Mark Hanna, August Belmont and J. P. Morgan, for the purpose of stabilizing labor relations. Gompers hoped to convince corporate management that satisfactory labor relations emerged from collective bargaining, and that unionization would not injure business prospects. Some influential business leaders seemed receptive to this argument. Their membership in the National Civic Federation encouraged Gompers to believe that the organization could further the acceptance of collective bargaining.

The strike, which later became the main weapon of organized labor, was another issue that produced much controversy in the post Civil War decade. Some labor leaders opposed the strike because it openly challenged the mutuality of interest doctrine. Journeymen, who soon hoped to become masters and employers, were slow to accept any device which sharply marked off the two groups and opened a type of warfare between them. Another important objection to the strike was the hostility it aroused in the general public. Some labor leaders argued that public support was essential if unions were to convince employers of the justice of their demands, and the strike alienated these potential allies.

Important as these considerations were, the opposition to strikes was most strongly influenced by the ineffectiveness of this weapon. Many strikes failed, even under favorable circumstances, and in difficult periods they were likely to be a disaster. Opponents charged that strikes embittered relations with the employer, led to the dismissal of workingmen, depleted a union's treasury, and placed hardships upon individual strikers—often for little or no gain (Source 18). The delegates to the national conventions of the trade unions discussed the strike frequently. While some union leaders opposed it, most argued that it was an essential method of insuring that the employer would respect his workers' interests. The proponents of the strike often argued that failures were the product of faulty planning and inadequate financing, and they called for a permanent strike fund to be dispensed by the national union (Source 19). This would give the national leaders more control over the timing of strikes, and it would allow them to offer adequate support (Source 20). Such a proposal roused the opposition of anti-strike unionists, plus those who jealously guarded the autonomy of locals. Few national strike funds were established during the 1860's and 1870's. In the 1880's, opposition within organized labor to the strike declined, and by the end of the century it had become the basic weapon of American trade unions.

The failure of many strikes and the general weakness of the trade unions help account for the switches in tactics that marked the post Civil War period. Economic conditions during the 1866 to 1868 years made trade union action difficult, and several major strikes failed, notably one conducted by the Iron Molders. These setbacks led many labor leaders to turn away from the use of traditional union methods. Monetary reform appealed to some, and new support arose for political action by organized labor. However, the most important device promoted in this brief period was producers' cooperation.

Proponents claimed that producers' cooperatives would allow workingmen to achieve the entrepreneurial position seemingly blocked by the increasing necessity for larger amounts of capital, the new importance of machinery, and the rapid breakdown of the apprenticeship system. Skilled workers could pool their savings in the cooperative shop, and thus achieve by collective means what they seemed unable to accomplish through individual effort (Source 21).

Certainly this interest in cooperation was, in part, a reaction to the failure of traditional trade union methods. But it was not entirely so. Before 1866, prominent labor leaders, such as William Sylvis, Richard Trevellick, and Thomas Phillips, supported cooperation as the ultimate means of ending the wage system and preventing the creation of a permanent working class in America. After 1868, many important labor spokesmen continued to press for more than the limited gains of trade unionism. On the other hand, most leaders of the printers, bricklayers and cigarmakers refused to give significant support, at any time, to cooperation, political action, or any other scheme that would turn the trade union from its function of protecting the worker by united economic action. These divisions in the labor movement exemplify the fluidity of thought in the 1860's as labor leaders sought the proper role for their organizations in the face of increasing industrialization.

The activities of the National Labor Union are one more example of these crosscurrents. The N.L.U., founded in 1866, placed increasing emphasis from 1866 to 1868 upon cooperation and monetary reform, thus reflecting the problems that beset trade unions at the time. Those temporarily estranged from economic action by trade unions, joined Sylvis and the others committed, in principle, to an attack upon the wage system. As prosperity returned to the nation in 1868, following the postwar depression, labor organizations found that strikes and other forms of economic action became more effective. Almost immediately, the N.L.U. began to lose the trade unionists attracted to it by desperation and despair. By 1870, the labor leaders and reformers who hoped to end the wage system completely dominated the National Labor Union, but the organization had lost its influence with trade unions that had now reembarked upon economic action. Its demise was not long in coming.

It was not uncommon to find trade union action combined with a basic desire to end the wage system. Sylvis was a successful trade union leader, who helped build the Iron Molders' International Union into one of the strongest labor organizations in the country. Yet Sylvis never viewed trade unionism as an end in itself. It protected the worker while he was a worker, educated him in united action, insured that he would be free of myths, such as identity of interest; but ultimately cooperation would provide the means for superseding the wage system. As Sylvis put it in his speech before the Iron Molders' International Union in 1864:

> Cooperation is the great idea of the age: it is the only means by which we can fully control both labor and money, by which we can secure to ourselves the wealth we have been so long creating for the use of others; for by it we secure a fair standard of wages, and a fair share of the profits arising from our industry.[25]

Uriah Stephens, the first leader of the Knights of Labor, also believed unionism had a role to play in protecting the worker, but that eventually it would be supplanted by the abolition of the wage system. The organization of the Knights was designed to serve this purpose: The local trade assembly acted much like a craft union, while the mixed district assembly was to be the vehicle for producers' cooperatives. It

[25] Ibid., p. 118.

was also possible for the leaders of an organization to favor cooperation while the rank and file concentrated on the protection of their interests through trade union action. This occurred in the Knights of St. Crispin, which organized shoemakers before 1873, and in the Knights of Labor during the 1880's.

As indicated, organized labor gave considerable attention to producers' cooperation during the late 1860's. Other elements within the nation also viewed cooperation quite favorably. Reformers interested in the "labor question" generally favored cooperation as a means of maintaining the dignity of the individual worker through mobility. They agreed with Sylvis and the other labor leaders who regarded the wage system as a danger to the traditional Jeffersonian concept of responsible manhood based on independent livelihood (Source 22). Strikes, and other forms of economic action by trade unions, were directed at individual employers, while cooperation produced no ugly strife, challenged employers through the sanctioned mechanism of the market, and yet contained the means for maintaining the mobility that industrialization seemed to threaten.

Many Americans were apprehensive about the increasing conflict between labor and capital. One reform organization, the National Guard of Industry—which was open to "All trustworthy persons who earn their bread by the sweat of their brow"—argued that

> While there exists neither reason nor necessity for antagonism between capital and labor, each being essential to the other, no fact is more patent than that capital, as now employed, is inimical to the interests of labor, and the working men's remedy is in co-operative industry, in possessing their own capital and employing their own labor. The history of co-operative enterprises for the last twenty-five years, both at home and abroad, demonstrates that the principle has passed beyond the domain of experiment into one of triumphant fact, and shows that it is entirely practicable to remove the disastrous antagonisms between capital and labor.[26]

Many employers also believed that cooperation had possibilities, for it provided an alternative to trade unionism, and the rate of failure among producers' cooperatives suggested that they were no real com-

---

[26] National Guard of Industry, *Platform and Subordinate Constitution* (Washington, D.C.: 1870), p. 4.

petitive threat. John Swinton, the perceptive labor editor, concisely summarized the attitude of the employer when he wrote that "As long as cooperative projects merely furnish by-play for a few men, they may be tolerated, but woe be them when they interfere with the profits or power of capital." [27] Since such a threat was usually remote, leading conservatives expressed enthusiasm for cooperation. They viewed it as another manifestation of the workingmen's desire to accept and prosper within the capitalist system.

The proponents of cooperation worked for it steadily, but labor leaders had generally lost interest by the 1880's. Even the reformers turned toward new approaches. Undoubtedly, the steady rate of failure for producers' cooperatives because of insufficient capital, poor management, strife among the cooperators, and the competition of long-established businesses convinced many that cooperation was not a viable alternative to trade unionism or some more effective reform program. However, it was still possible during the depression of the mid-eighties to rouse the delegates to the Cigar Makers' International Union convention of 1885 to approve a resolution that declared: "[The] complete emancipation of labor cannot take place until the laborer is no longer dependent upon the individual for the right to work." The Convention then recommended "some steps looking towards the erection of cooperative cigar factories if found practicable." [28] President Adolph Strasser, a stout opponent of cooperation, never found such a proposal practicable. However, the resolution shows the vague appeal of producers' cooperatives, even in this bastion of trade unionism, given some disillusionment with economic action because of the depression.

The question of political action also divided the ranks of organized labor (Source 23). Supporters of monetary reform or shorter hours believed that political action was indispensable. Some cooperationists also favored political action, but leaders such as Uriah Stephens and Terence V. Powderly believed that labor's own organizations could be the basis for producers' cooperatives, and that involvement in politics was unnecessary and divisive. The supporters of economic action by trade unions basically accepted the functioning capitalist system, and to them political action was perhaps the greatest snare. It was, in fact, a threat to the

---

[27] *John Swinton's Paper* (July 5, 1885), 1.
[28] Cigar Makers' International Union, *Proceedings* (1885), p. 19.

very existence of organized labor. Experience in the antebellum years had demonstrated that American workers were divided among the major and minor parties, and that any attempt to marshal them in support of one party or candidate, through the trade union, was more likely to fracture the union than to elect the candidate. Furthermore, joint action with reformers had often submerged the union's economic functions beneath the broader program of the political movement, with the result that the almost inevitable collapse of the reform party dragged down the labor organizations as well. Political action was not basic to labor leaders who accepted the fundamental structure of society and merely demanded protection and progress within it.

This did not mean that trade unionists ignored all political action. However, political activities were supplementary to the economic methods of the union, and they were usually limited to pressure for specific legislation, such as the exclusion of contract labor or Chinese immigrants, the abolition of labor by prisoners in state institutions, the prohibition of manufacturing in tenements, and, in some cases, legislative enactment of a ten-hour or eight-hour law. Obviously, organized labor's influence upon legislators rested on the potentialities of the "labor vote," but this vote rarely materialized for any period of time, and never on the national level.

Extraordinary strains, or climactic and stirring events, might lead organized labor to support political campaigns at the state and local level. Thus, there was a flurry of political activity in 1877 and 1878 as a result of the long depression and the Railroad Strike of 1877. The depression had destroyed many trade unions, and the violence connected with the Railroad Strike had liberated a torrent of anti-labor sentiment among conservatives. The depression of 1883 to 1886 and the Haymarket Affair help explain the participation of labor organizations in political campaigns during 1886 and 1887. At the local level, candidates supported by labor bodies achieved some success, especially in periods of great excitement. However, most trade unions carefully avoided any permanent commitment to a party, and many chose not even to act for or against a specific candidate, leaving this to city central labor councils or state federations that did not carry out economic activities. National trade unions rarely took a stand on national elections, fearing that such a step would disrupt the unity of the membership.

By the 1880's, most labor leaders accepted the wage system, and thus there was a corresponding decline in the appeal of political action designed to supersede the effects of industrialization. Organized labor flirted with the Populists in the 1890's, but it was on the basis of the acceptance of the worker's fixed position. Most labor leaders opposed political action for all the old reasons; but they also stressed that the objectives of the Populists were the traditional ones of the small entrepreneur, and these no longer had an attraction for labor leaders who had given up the mobility objectives of the success ethic. William Trant put the point well in a pamphlet widely distributed by the A.F.L.:

> The object of a trade union is a wide one, viz., to do all that can be done to better in every respect the conditions of its members. . . . Unlike most kinds of individual effort, the object is not to assist men to lift themselves out of their class, as if they were ashamed of it, or as if manual labor were a disgrace, but to raise the class itself in physical well-being and self-estimation.[29]

Gompers' insistence upon the specific interests of the industrial workers flatly opposed a basic premise of the political activists. Labor leaders and reformers opposed to the wage system generally supported some sort of producing class concept which united farmers, workingmen, and small entrepreneurs in one group with a common set of interests. The enemy became the trusts, banks, railroads, and other representatives of great wealth (Source 24). As the editor of The Guardian of New York explained in 1872:

> It has hitherto been the favorite policy of capital, the chief cause of all the trouble, to sit back in its velvet chair and chuckle over the contest between laborer and employer, when, in truth, the real ground for the fight should be between capital on one side and employers and employed, hand in hand, on the other side.[30]

The great capitalists were attacked for attempting to shatter the old American system, based on individual mobility through an open society, in order to replace it with a permanent working class, fixed for-

[29] William Trant, Trade Unions: Their Origin and Objects, Influence and Efficacy (New York: American Federation of Labor, 1888), p. 14.
[30] The Guardian (January 27, 1872), 92.

ever in the relative poverty of the small farm, the factory, or the workshop. Any distinction between rural and urban interests seemed slight since the success ethic argued for movement from farm to town as well as from employee to entrepreneur.

This unity was never achieved, and by the late 1870's the Greenbackers were using the producing class doctrine to win support for an inflationism which was not a central concern of urban workingmen. The Populists made a more intensive effort to create a political party based upon the producing class doctrine, but they achieved little success. Most labor leaders of the 1890's no longer viewed workers as part of a producing class, but as a distinctive group that should seek its best interests primarily through economic action.

Monetary reform, centering around the issuance of greenbacks, also gained considerable support from labor leaders and reformers in the 1860's and 1870's. Many labor leaders were attracted to the theories of Edward Kellogg and Alexander Campbell, who argued that the issuance of paper currency would force down interest rates and increase business activity. Campbell believed that a national greenback currency should be convertible at the option of the holder into government bonds. These bonds would bear three per cent interest and they would be convertible into greenbacks. Campbell thought this plan would prevent the depreciation of the paper money and would block the centralization of wealth in the hands of the few who controlled the supply of capital (Source 25). The National Labor Union adopted this plan as one of its major proposals.

William Sylvis argued in 1868 that a reduction in the rate of interest, and the issuance of greenbacks, would mean that "new enterprises will be started, machinery now idle will be put in motion; there will be work for all and peace and plenty will bless the land." [31] On the other hand, high interest rates, produced by an inflexible, relatively meagre money supply, enriched the bankers but handicapped productive enterprises that employed labor. This kind of argument naturally had its greatest appeal in depressions, such as 1866–1868, or the years following 1873. John James, the Secretary of the Miners' National Association, saw a clear connection between the currency supply and depressions. He favored a Greenback Party which would:

[31] Sylvis, *Speeches*, pp. 382–383.

. . . produce such a condition of things by financial legislation as will necessarily make employment plenty and at good wages to the workman. . . . It aims to furnish for the people a currency—a medium of exchange—that will in the future prevent the panics made by interested capitalists and save the people from such pinching times as presently prevail.[32]

Most greenbackers concentrated upon the salutary effects of paper money on the existing economic system. They stressed that monetary reform would provide an adequate supply of currency, insuring that the maximum number of jobs possible would be available. It would also erase the dips in the business cycle, which were blamed upon the improper management of capital by the bankers. In addition, it would make more funds available to the small entrepreneur and the farmer. Some supporters of paper money believed an adequate currency would also enable producers' cooperatives to secure capital more easily, thus contributing to the battle against a permanent working class.

The attraction of monetary reform was wide in the 1860's and 1870's, but even in this period, those labor leaders who relied primarily on the economic activities of the trade union ignored greenback schemes. They distrusted the independent political action that the greenbackers called for, while some retained the distrust of paper money that had marked labor organizations in the antebellum period. In the 1880's, the greenbackers continued to stress a producers' class doctrine and the universal benefits of paper money, but the movement declined among all portions of the public except the farmers. Organized labor gave it very little support.

In contrast to monetary reform, labor leaders were united in their support of proposals for an eight-hour day. The influence of Ira Steward of Boston upon the agitation for the eight-hour day was most remarkable. Although labor leaders rejected many of his methods, including his strong belief that any widespread reduction in hours had to come through political action, they embraced his basic theory warmly. Steward was a leader in the campaigns for an eight-hour day during the 1860's, and in the 1880's and 1890's his theory still was the basis for the A.F.L.'s commitment to a shorter work day.

Steward believed that wages depend upon the standard of living,

[32] Labor Standard (New York) (October 7, 1876), 2.

and that fewer hours of work would generate more wants as men sought to use their leisure most fully. Therefore, wages would rise to meet the new standard of expectations, and production would expand to meet the new markets. Employers would find that higher wages generated more demand and higher profits. Steward and the A.F.L. agreed further that increased leisure would permit workers to educate themselves and learn their interests and rights more fully. Greater unity and more effective action by workingmen would result. Steward finally concluded that this greater self-development and education would make workers realize their precarious situation under the wage system, and eventually shorter hours would lead to a demand from the rank and file laborers and mechanics for producers' and consumers' cooperatives. The A.F.L. ignored this final element of Steward's theory (Source 26).

Steward's program had a wide appeal among those reformers who wanted to block the hardening class lines and the increased dependency of workingmen upon their employers. The eight-hour day was a concrete measure that could rally support from workingmen and labor organizations, yet it was based upon the mutuality of interest so dear to reformers in the 1860's. Moreover, it ultimately promised to further producers' cooperatives. Although labor unions opposed Steward's emphasis upon the eight-hour day as an alternative to trade unionism, they often were willing to cooperate with reformers during the 1860's in campaigns for the eight-hour legislation. To the trade union, eight hours was the objective; to the reformer, it was merely the beginning.

Some workingmen opposed the reduction of hours because they feared a proportionate reduction of wages. Government officials and employers argued continuously that the two would have to go together, despite Steward's claims that shorter hours would increase profits. The eight-hour laws that were passed in the late 1860's proved to be so full of loopholes that they became ineffective. Furthermore, government officials often ignored the laws that set the eight-hour day in their departments. A witness before a House Committee that investigated the depression of the 1870's pinpointed the reason for this disregard for the law:

> They would not be able to violate it if there was public opinion to back up the law. . . . The law would be obeyed if it was not in advance of public sentiment. I am sorry to say that the public is less

intelligent in that direction than the framers and promoters of the law.[33]

Such public support for meaningful, widespread regulation of the hours of adult men did not appear until the 1930's. Through experience, labor leaders learned that only a strong trade union could secure and enforce eight hours without a reduction in pay. Therefore, the unions of the 1880's shunned cooperation with reformers of the Steward stripe; instead they sought the eight-hour day by direct economic pressure upon the employer.

We have noted that the 1880's marked the decline of sentiment within organized labor for an eventual end of the wage system through the advance of workers into the entrepreneurial ranks. However, one must be careful not to conclude that such sentiments died suddenly. On the contrary, one finds that producers' cooperation still attracted significant support; that the producing class idea was still strong enough in 1884 to lead the Illinois Federation of Labor to invite the State Grange to participate in its first state convention; and that the Knights of Labor was still controlled by leaders who opposed the idea of a relatively immobile working class.

The multitudes who entered the Knights in 1884 and 1885, and the strongly entrenched trade union elements within the organization, paid little heed to the doctrine of the national leaders. This conflict in objective between the national leadership and much of the membership badly weakened the Knights. Thus the *Cigar Makers' Journal* pointed out in 1883 that "Perhaps the loudest in their denunciation of strikes are the Knights of Labor and upon investigation we discover that they are all the time striking." [34] The Constitution of the Knights stated that "Strikes, at best, only afford temporary relief, and members should be educated to depend upon thorough organization, co-operation and political action and through these the abolishment of the wage system." [35]

---

[33] United States House of Representatives, *Investigation by a Select Committee of The House of Representatives Relative to the Causes of the General Depression in Labor and Business; and as to Chinese Immigration* (Washington, D.C.: Government Printing Office, 1879), pp. 435–36.

[34] *Cigar Makers' Journal*, VIII (July 1883), 4.

[35] Knights of Labor of America, *Constitutions of the General Assembly, and for the State, National, Trade, District, and Local Assemblies* (Washington, D.C.: 1887), p. 40.

Despite this provision, and the many statements by Powderly against strikes, pressure from the membership forced consideration of a national strike fund. Eventually, most trade unions abandoned the Knights, not only because of the reverses experienced in 1886 and 1887, but also because membership as an affiliate of the A.F.L. was more in agreement with their basic aims.

There were also contradictory forces at work within the other elements of organized labor. Gompers believed that class consciousness was essential if workers were to be united. Yet the most highly skilled workers, such as railroad engineers and skilled steel workers, retained a strong hope for individual advancement into supervisory positions. They tended to ignore class consciousness. The union had to defend the worker while he was a worker, but constant attention turned to promotion out of the ranks of the workingmen. Their unions thus developed a blend of protective trade unionism and belief in individual mobility.

To a lesser extent, this dualism was also present in most of American, non-socialist trade unionism. Even as labor leaders preached class consciousness, they did not fully accept the obvious corollary of a fixed class structure. Instead they argued for class consciousness, but allowed for the possibility of mobility. However, it was stressed that most workers would not leave the wage-earning ranks, and thus the trade union had the obligation to use collective action to guarantee these workingmen a fair share in the increasing wealth of the nation. Moreover, a worker's complete commitment to the success ethic frequently made him hostile or apathetic to trade unionism, and labor leaders stressed that this was self-defeating. The *Cigar Makers' Journal* could well state that "the labor movement is a war against poverty. It is a true leveler. It levels up."[36] Yet the workingman was usually more interested in his own upward mobility than in class movement to a higher level. American unions had to respond to both of these elements.

Throughout this period, a group of middle- and upper-class social critics and reformers proposed to speak for and to the American workingman concerning his best interests. Most of these critics in the 1860's and 1870's were supporters of a fancied older order of self-employed master craftsmen, small employers, and yeomen farmers, and they re-

[36] *Cigar Makers' Journal,* VI (1881), 1.

garded the creation of a permanent industrial work force as a disaster. Almost without exception, they attacked the increase in the number of large corporations and the appearance of immense personal fortunes. Yet these critics almost always opposed a redistribution of property to meet the problems of the nation; instead they concentrated on measures that would insure a more equitable distribution of income in the future, through some system other than the industrial wage order. They were clearly more concerned with equity than equality.

The reformers were the strongest supporters of producers' cooperation and a new monetary system, and they played an important role in the eight-hour movement of the late 1860's. These measures were viewed as steps toward an eventual end of the wage system. Government action was necessary for those who demanded monetary reform, and it soon became the weapon of the Eight-Hour Leagues. However, most co-operationists did not emphasize legislation, and generally the reformers did not call for reform through continuous government action. Instead limited steps by government were expected to keep the avenues for individual advancement open so that men could work at decent wages during reasonable hours, secure property, and hopefully become entrepreneurs.

Trade unionists opposed to the development of a relatively immobile working class readily cooperated with the reformers, but many other labor leaders were cool toward them. This latter group of union leaders opposed the reformers' stress upon mobility for the individual; they feared the growth of any organization that could become a challenge to the trade union; and they objected to the air of superiority exhibited by many reformers. These upper- or middle-class critics often adopted a tone that urged workingmen to follow the lead of their intellectual and social betters, and they often claimed to know better than the worker himself what was in his best interests.

The social critics could not be ignored, for they might have greater access to public opinion, and more significant influence with legislators and important government officials, than did organized labor itself. Thus an uneasy relationship developed between organized labor and the social reformers. Organized labor needed the support of reform-minded individuals and organizations, but it was determined not to become subservient to any outside group.

The 1880's witnessed a change in attitude among reformers that closely paralleled the developments among labor leaders. There was an increasing acceptance of the fixity of the worker's position, which made the doctrines of the 1860's and 1870's obsolete. Workers would generally remain workers, and if their lot were to be improved, it would have to be through trade unionism or legislation. Most reformers preferred to use legislation as the vehicle for change (Source 27). They were quite uneasy about trade unionism since the labor organizations showed a constant determination to serve the interests of their members, even should the reformers object to the course of action. Conversely, reformers believed their influence was likely to be greater with legislators and government officials than with trade union leaders. Also, legislation seemed able to reach more workers in a more uniform way, though the reliance on state, rather than national, action reduced the scope of the legislation that was passed and created new groups of favored workers, not unlike the advantaged workmen served by strong trade unions.

Labor leaders were wary of legislation for many of the same reasons that led the reformers to favor it. The trade union leader was quite conscious of his differences with the reformers, and with the incomparably greater gap between himself and the average legislator. Thus he was reluctant to submit to their views of what the worker's interests should be. For these labor leaders, strong organization promised more to the workers than legislation, especially in light of the ineffectiveness of most of organized labor's political efforts. This question disturbed the relations between reformers and trade union leaders until the 1930's. It also produced sharp splits within the labor movement.

The reformers were prepared to admit the inadequate living conditions of many workingmen and to demand changes. However, they considered these changes within the broader concept of a just society, in which labor reform was one element that had to fit with others. For many reformers, unionism deserved support because organized labor might be an ally in the battle for other elements of the reform program. If labor leaders refused such an alliance, friction resulted. Other reformers reluctantly admitted that the worker could not defend his interests against the large corporation without united action. However, they were often opposed to a union's tactics—including strikes and the closed shop—as well as to elements of the union's program, and thus support for the principle of unionism was often tempered by disapproval of the specific actions of unions. The reformers of the 1880's and 1890's increasingly operated on different premises from the social critics of two decades earlier; however, this did not resolve the tension between themselves and the labor leaders.

By 1896, the changing position of the worker in industrial America had led most reformers and labor leaders to give up on the success ethic. Twentieth-century labor reform and trade unionism were to proceed from this point. The commitment to mobility for the worker had not been easily abandoned since the success ethic was one of the strongest elements in American popular thought and an important buttress of the established social order. As we have seen, the general public, including great numbers of workingmen, continued to believe in this doctrine. The strength of this widely accepted attitude limited the success of reformers and labor unions alike, and it was surely one of the most important influences upon the conditions of life and labor in late nineteenth-century America.

Are We in Danger of Revolution?

J. L. Spalding

This statement contains the major elements of the success ethic, but Spalding also finds it necessary to defend the great capitalists—an indication of the increasing attacks upon them. His emphasis on the opportunities open to the immigrant should be compared with Sources 5–10. Spalding was Bishop of Peoria, Illinois, from 1877 to 1908, and one of the leading Catholic commentators on social and labor affairs. Although the success ethic was often identified with Protestant thought and values, this selection indicates its appeal to a prominent Catholic spokesman.

How quickly the angry passions of our Civil War have sunk to rest, however much demagogues have sought to keep them alive. No hatred can long flourish here. The poor do not hate the rich, and the rich as a body are not indifferent to the wants of the poor. Our wealthy men are the children of the poor, and their children or grandchildren will either perish utterly or go to work again with the laboring masses. Thus the money line, which is really the only line with us that separates class from class, is not a fixed boundary dividing hostile armies. We have, after all, but a sprinkling of very rich men, who have their uses, even when they are unintelligent and narrowminded, or personally worthless. Capital is the army of a commercial age, and capitalists are necessary to undertake and carry on great enterprises; they fill the places of the captains of warlike ages. A railroad king may inflict financial ruin upon individuals and be unjust to his employees, but he will develop the country and bring material blessings to thousands. Even stock-waterers and railway-wreckers probably do far more good than harm to the general public. But the great capitalists, as I have said, are few, and in America pauperism is accidental. The people are neither

J. L. Spalding, "Are We in Danger of Revolution?" *The Forum*, I (July 1886), 407–8.

paupers nor millionaires, but workers, whose energy and thrift secure them a competence. Seven millions, seven hundred and fifty thousand of these are farmers, while only about half this number are engaged in manufacturing. Three-fourths of these farmers own the land they cultivate, and the general tendency is to diminish rather than to increase the size of farms. Our laborers, too, receive higher wages and live in greater plenty than those of any other country. The story of our material progress reads like a dream, and we, who are now living, see but the beginnings of this incomprehensible work, and in many other respects our course is forward. Each generation begins the life-struggle from a higher plain. The multitudes who arrive here from Europe feel the quickening influence of our life, and their nobler faculties awaken. Thousands each year revisit their native lands and feel like strangers there, so thoroughly have they become imbued with the American spirit. They are not only satisfied with our political institutions, but find it difficult to imagine that they were ever able to bear the shackles and restraints of less liberal governments. If ours is the country of rich men, why do the poor, from the ends of the earth, flock to our shores? If capitalists exercise here a tyrannic power, why do the oppressed of every land seek refuge with us? In truth, we occupy the foremost position among the free nations of the world, and wherever political development is taking place it is in the direction in which we are leading. Our people either know this or feel it instinctively, and they really have no fears at all as to the fortune of the Republic.

source 2

"I Ain't Going to Learn a Trade!"

William Oland Bourne

> The *Iron Platform* was a weekly journal of comment on current problems edited by the poet and essayist, William Oland Bourne. He issued the *Extra* as a monthly supplement, intended for a wider audience including workingmen. Bourne belonged to that group of northern Democrats who supported the Civil War in order to maintain the Union, and he vigorously sought to influence workingmen to support this position. Bourne accepted the success ethic, and the selection indicates his support for the dignity traditionally linked with skilled labor. Compare this statement with Source 3 written over three decades later.

Not long ago a boy was about leaving school, and as I had a chance to speak to him, I asked, "What are you going to do?" "I am going into a merchant's jobbinghouse." "Going to be a clerk, then. Why do you not learn a trade?" "Trade!" said he, *"I ain't going to learn a trade!"*

"Not going to learn a trade. I should like to know why a trade is not as good as a clerkship. I suppose you think it is more genteel and respectable! What would you do if nobody learned a trade? Where would you be with your *jobbing-house,* I wonder. Now, if you would only be a bookbinder, or printer, or carpenter, or mason, or shoemaker, and act with the true spirit of a noble workman, you may reach the head of your business, and become the best known man in your line in the whole country."

"What, be a *cobbler?*"

"Certainly. You had better be a good cobbler, and a successful man in your character and life, than a bad clerk or a doubtful merchant. Have you never heard of men that have learned trades, and what they have done? Now, suppose I and my brother, and Mr. Johnson, and

Iron Platform, Extra (October 1861), p. 4.

Mr. White, and a good many others, go to work at our trades, and we make boots, shoes, hats, tin pans, knives, threshing mills, watches, and other things, and then, because you have never learned a trade, and *don't know enough* to be of any other use to us, suppose we ask you to sell these for us—how much more genteel are you than we? Is it genteel to earn a living in some way, without being obliged to take off your coat and dirty your hands? It may be *genteel* in one sense, but the clerk who begins in that spirit will pretty surely make a *bad merchant*. The merchant or the clerk who will not take off his coat, and lift a bale of goods, or nail up a box, but makes the porter do it, because it is beneath him, may get along in the world, but the chances are against him.

"Learn a trade! Did you never hear of such a man as Ben Franklin, who learned the printing trade, and became one of the most distinguished men of modern times? Have you never heard of a carpenter named Rittenhouse, or a man who made philosophical instruments and afterwards revolutionized the world with his discoveries in the steam engine? Have you heard of James Watt, or is it *genteel* not to know any thing about trades or those who have learned them? Who was Arkwright, that followed the trade of a barber? Or, Whitney, or Fulton? Who was Governor Armstrong, of Massachusetts, or Isaac Hill, of New Hampshire, who learned the trade of a printer. Did you ever hear of the man who swung his sledge at the anvil, and became the distinguished blacksmith, named Elihu Burritt? And talking about cobblers, did you ever hear of a distinguished cobbler named Roger Sherman? Or of the illustrious lame cobbler of London named John Pounds, who founded Ragged Schools, and put into operation one of the greatest pieces of moral machinery of the age."

"No! "

"You haven't? Well you know just enough to be a clerk? You should feel it to be an honor to stand on the same platform with such men, even if they are distinguished cobblers and blacksmiths.

"But go on! Be wise! *Resolve to do always* as well as you know how! Be faithful and persevere! By and by we shall perhaps hear of your being a distinguished merchant—distinguished for private and public virtue."

So we bade our young friend good bye, with our best wishes, and resolved to say to our readers in the IRON PLATFORM, about the same as we said to him.

About the Would-Be Dude
Who Hates to Be Called
a Workingman

William Strauss

This article was published in the official journal of the Journeymen
Tailors' Union of America, which was affiliated with the A.F.L.
Sources 2 and 3 illustrate the problem of organizing workers who
were strongly attracted to the success ethic.

Is it not remarkable that notwithstanding the rapid progress
organized labor is making in all parts of the country, there are yet a
considerable number of supposedly intelligent and liberal-minded men
right here in this land of the free who are of the opinion that their
belonging to or being in any way associated with a labor organization
would result in a lowering of their dignity and social standing; that
their position in "society" would be materially affected were it generally
known that they were identified with any movement having the un-
dignified title of *labor* attached to it? Now this statement becomes the
more remarkable when we consider the fact that these same individuals
are not men enjoying life on the prudent investment of their surplus
capital, but are in most instances working for a salary so low as to be
beneath even the consideration of the average mechanic. This is a true
statement of facts. There are hundreds of men in different branches of
industry in this city who from a want of appreciation of the benefits of
a labor organization, are absolutely at the mercy of employers who are
not at all times just and considerate in their treatment of employees.
But who is responsible for this unpleasant state of affairs? Certainly

The Tailor, VII (August 1896), 9.

not the employers but the employees themselves. Try to interest one of them by an explanation of the protection afforded his interests through affiliating with a labor organization, and he immediately assumes an air of cold indifference. But mention to him an organization of the social club order, where political debates, occasional hops, entertainments, and receptions are principal features, and he is all attention at once. This suits him exactly; it is most appropriate, for in institutions of this kind he can preserve his social dignity and be separate and distinct from that class of individuals he contemptuously designates as "workingmen." Now, if there ever was a case of pure, unadulterated inconsistency we have it here. Just fancy a man earning the princely salary of a few dollars per week who would prefer being a member of a social club as outlined above rather than belong to a labor organization. Just for the sake of argument let us compare the two.

It cannot be denied that the advantages of the club from a social standpoint are many, but are these advantages of more importance to the wage-earner than those he derives from his labor organization? We think not. The labor organization is a school wherein a man is taught the great principles of friendship, brotherly love, and honesty of purpose, wherein by a constant exchange of ideas his views of men and things become more broad and liberal. He is taught to be unselfish, to care for the interest and welfare of his fellow men as well as for himself, and to promote and advance the cause of civilization in general.

Such are the principles on which labor organizations are founded, and the man who is a member of one feels assured that in his hour of distress his brother members will lend him a helping hand, feels assured of their protection, and earns not only the confidence and respect of his fellow workman, but the esteem and respect of his employer also. And now as to the dignity of labor itself. We are of the opinion that all grades of labor, no matter how menial or subservient if honestly performed, can justly claim the title of dignity. What material difference does it make whether a man earns his salary measuring out ribbon behind a counter all day long or hammering out a livelihood on an anvil; the humble carpenter who hammers nails and saws wood for a living— all things being equal—is just as much worth our friendship and esteem as the haughty bank cashier or the autocratic railroad superintendent. We have good reason to be proud that we are identified with labor, for is not labor responsible for all things with which we are surrounded, from that ancient and substantial monument of human industry and patience, the great wall of China, down to that modern triumph of engineering skill as displayed in the Brooklyn bridge. Have we not in the delicate touches with which the great Messonier almost gave life to his canvas, priceless treasures with which to show future generations what artistic labor can do? Have we not evidence of brain labor in every pathetic appeal, in every flash of eloquence delivered by that prince of labor orators, Eugene V. Debs, and no one will dispute that years of incessant labor were represented in Jenner's great discovery of inoculation. So that on all sides we see the results of labor and feel that without labor of some kind nothing can be accomplished. It is the all important factor in the world's progress, and the man who seeks to detract from its dignity, or who is ashamed to own his connection with it, leaves himself open to the ridicule and contempt of all classes of right-thinking men, and justly so. The immortal Abe Lincoln was always pleased to refer to the fact that at one period of his checkered career he was an unknown, hard-working backwoodsman. The lamented General Garfield began life as a canal boy, and honest and manly Andy Johnson felt flattered upon being reminded that the political plans he formulated while at work on the tailor's bench led to his occupying the Presidential chair in the White House as chief magistrate of this great country.

So you see, my friends, there is nothing to be ashamed of in connection with labor. Give up at once your exalted ideas. This is the age of practice, not theory. If there is no organization of members of your calling, interest yourself in starting one, after which, if you feel so inclined, you may go into "society," feeling that you have done your duty —not only to yourself but to your fellow man.

source 4

Mobility and the Common Man

Richard Ely

> Ely was perhaps the best known of the "New Economists" who
> challenged accepted principles in many areas of social and economic
> thought. He was influenced by the developing social gospel, and, in
> turn, his work had an important influence on many leaders in the
> campaigns for social reform that were part of the Progressive move-
> ment.

Trades-unions and other associations of laborers are designed to
protect and advance the interest of the great mass of the working classes.
They are intended primarily for the average man, and not for those with
extraordinary economic capacities. The latter class may occasionally find
them useful, but usually men possessed of economic gifts of a higher
order wish no help from labor organizations. They desire a free course,
and ask to be let alone. There can be no more useful person in the
community than the talented man, provided he is at the same time a
man obedient to the dictates of practical ethics; and it is desirable that
his freedom of movement should not be restrained, so long as he does
not intrench upon the liberties of his neighbor, or does not otherwise
injure his fellow-men. It will at times happen that the cheapest man
in a town is the "captain of industry," whose unusual abilities yield
him an annual income of twenty, thirty, or forty thousand dollars per
annum; and by saying that he is the cheapest man in the town, I mean
that he renders greater service to the community for every dollar received than any one else. Though it is often necessary to put a check on
greed, and to restrain the activity of the unscrupulous, the true policy
for all social classes, and therefore for society as a whole, is to encourage
the development of talent.

Richard Ely, *The Labor Movement in America* (New York: Thomas Y.
Crowell and Co., 1886), pp. 92–95.

But one of the elementary truths which we in this country specially
need to grasp is that the average man is not a peculiarly gifted man.
What do we mean by able, talented, and such expressions? By them
we call attention to the fact that a man is superior to the vast majority.
The terms are relative, and as ordinarily used they can no more apply
to all men than two and two can make five. This is simple; but nothing
is more fraught with weighty consequences, and nothing is oftener overlooked in discussions of social problems. How common is the saying,
"There is always plenty of room on the top shelf," or "in the upper
story." What of it? All men can no more get there than every tree in
the forest can be taller than all the other trees. Yet people talk as if this
were possible. The extreme of this absurdity is seen in the traditional
elderly gentleman who tells all the boys in the village school that they
may one day become President of the United States. Though doubtless
spoken in ignorance, it is, in the nature of things, a falsehood. Let us,
then, begin any treatment of the labor question, or any other social
problem, with a frank recognition of the fact that we have to deal with
the ninety-nine out of a hundred who by no human possibility can
ascend to the "upper story." One hundred men may struggle ever so
hard; but if they are to have only one leader, only one can rise to that
position of eminence. You may urge them on and render the struggle
severer, but the ultimate result is the same. Take the case of independent
producers. The relative number of those who belong to that class has
been steadily diminishing for years, as production on a large scale has
taken the place of the small shop. It lies, then, in the nature of things,
that under our present industrial system the relative portion of wage-
receivers in manufactories must increase. It is not the fault of the
laborer; it is not the fault of their employers. When one begins to dis-
cuss the labor question, one often hears the remark, "The majority of
rich manufacturers began themselves as poor boys. They were once
employees." The statement itself would not bear such close scrutiny as
some might think, for it is not so true of an old country as of a new;
not so true of the manufacturers of forty years of age as of those of
seventy. But if we accept the statement, what of it? What bearing has
that on the condition of those who remain journeymen all their lives?
Is not your self-made man—who, as Horace Greeley said, is sometimes
too inclined to worship his own creator—often the most haughty, over-
bearing, and tyrannical? Not always; for nobler men do not live than

some of these. But too often it is true, and the laborer whose master was once a workingman himself has then cause to regret it. It ought at the same time to be remarked, that where one laborer rises to the position of a wealthy man, ten small producers have lost their independent positions and fallen into the rank of wage-receivers. The gradual disappearance of the village carpenter, the village shoemaker, and others of that class, is a fact well known in our own East; and in older countries, the distress of the once large and flourishing class of small masters working with two or three journeymen has given rise to a social problem.

Let us allude to another allied fallacy. The newspapers tell us that the sons of rich men squander their property and fall into the ranks of poor people; and this is repeated again and again as if it ought to allay anxiety about the future. Most happily the statement is only exceptionally true; but if it were the unfortunate state of affairs, how could it solve any social problem?

Let us put away all these shallow sophistries. What we want in this country is to know how to improve the laboring man as a laboring man—for such the great mass must remain for many years to come, and it may be safe to say for generations to come, whatever unknown conditions a future social development may bring us. To elevate the farmer as a farmer, the mechanic as a mechanic, the artisan as an artisan, in short, to lift the entire "Fourth Estate," as it is called, should be the effort of public reform and private philanthropy. It is not our public schools in themselves which turn our youth away from manual occupations, but the cry "rise in life" which fills the air and which leads to false estimates of human worthiness. Truly, every one should attempt to "rise in life" in the correct meaning of those words, but our schoolbooks, our periodicals for the young, and, one might almost say, our entire literature, all are carrying to our young people throughout the length and breadth of the land the conception that to rise in life means to become a great manufacturer, a railway president, or a merchant prince. No wonder that humble toil is scorned.

Attacks on the Immigrant

Sources 5 and 6 illustrate the major arguments used by those anxious to restrict immigration. The New York Association for Improving the Condition of the Poor was a major private charitable organization. Edward Bemis was a well-known authority on public utilities, a faculty member at several universities, and a member of Tom Johnson's reform administration in Cleveland during the years 1901–1909. Bemis' attitude toward the immigrant exemplifies the thinking of a large number of reformers who feared that the increasing tide of immigration would constitute a threat to effective political reform and a menace to improvements in the living and working conditions of labor.

A MASS OF IGNORANCE, VICE, AND HEATHENISM

The New York Association for Improving the Condition of the Poor

The City of New York has the largest number of foreigners, though not the largest ratio compared with the residue of the population, and while it is admitted that many of them become very desirable and estimable citizens, it must also be conceded that a large proportion in this and other of our eastern cities are, as respects intelligence and character, far inferior to the average of the native-born. Experience, moreover, has uniformly shown that such immigrants as have pecuniary means, industry, and enterprise, mostly seek homes in the interior, pressing onward to the north-west, and some, latterly, diverging to the Southern States, where they become valuable acquisitions, while the

The New York Association for Improving the Condition of the Poor, *Annual Report*, No. 24 (1867), pp. 37–40.

61

thriftless, the ignorant, and degraded, generally lodge, like driftwood, where they land, to fill our prisons, and burden our charities. As an indication of their lack of culture and low grade of civilization, official statistics show, that of the persons over twenty-one years of age in this city, who cannot read and write, there are about twenty foreigners to one native. In other words, while there are but 1,200 natives over twenty-one years of age who can neither read nor write, there are 40,580 of the foreign-born over that age who cannot read the English language. Is it, therefore, surprising that most of the social and political evils in the city, may be traced to the ignorance and debasement of our immigrant population?

It may be further remarked, that the native-born, which comprise more than half the inhabitants, give about twenty-three per cent of our city indigence; the foreign-born, including those aided by the Commissioners of Emigration, amount to seventy-seven per cent, which is nearly four imported paupers for one American. The statistics of crime exhibit results as marked and striking. Of the 68,873 persons arrested for offences against person and property, for the year ending October 31st, 1865,—45,837 were foreigners; and of these 32,867 were Irish, and but 23,036—white and black, all told, were natives. Of the whole number arrested, 13,576 could neither read nor write. Nor should the fact be overlooked, that many of the native-born paupers and criminals are the offspring of foreigners, who were themselves paupers and criminals. Hence, much of our indigenous pauperism and crime is mediately traceable to foreign parentage, which, under our genial institutions, produces and perpetuates this noxious and parasitic growth of unproductive humanity.

Again—what class of our citizens must strenuously resist the moral restraints of the community, when irreconcilable with their own habits, and factiously combine to defeat the operation of the most benign laws, when they happen to oppose their own demoralizing indulgences, or supposed interests? Who among our population would give unrestricted and unregulated license to the ten thousand drinking places in the city, which are the chief receptacles of drunkenness, debauchery, villainy, and disease? Who is it that would annihilate the Sabbath—the very citadel of Christian institutions—the bulwark of private virtue, domestic happiness, national freedom, and prosperity—by converting it into a day of profligacy and dissipation? To these, and similar interrogations, which might be indefinitely multiplied, let facts respond, and there is but one answer.

All who are conversant with the social and moral condition of this city will admit, that there is now, in the lower strata of the population, a larger mass of ignorance, vice, and heathenism combined, than was ever before known in our history. Its chief source is familiar to us. It is the residuum or dregs of four millions of European immigrants, including paupers, felons, and convicts, that have landed at this port within the last twenty years. Uncultured [and] credulous, they brought with them the habits, prejudices, passions, and vices of the Old World. Brutalized by oppression at home, they had grown into the habit of regarding law as their enemy, the rich as their tyrants and lawful prey. Suddenly transferred to a country where the law imposes no test either of intelligence or education for the exercise of the suffrage, they are soon enfranchised, and admitted to all the rights and privileges of citizenship. The significance of such enfranchisement is shown by the fact that, out of the 120,000 voters in the City of New York, about 77,000, it is computed, or nearly two-thirds of the whole number, are chiefly drawn from the most ignorant and degraded classes of European society. Such a constituency, requiring, of course, a corresponding representation, created a description of political leaders before unknown in our municipal government—cunning, shrewd, unscrupulous demagogues, intent mainly on their own selfish greed—among whom those were ever most popular and successful who pandered most adroitly to the foibles, vices, and prejudices of the masses. That the government of the city, under these circumstances, should pass into their hands, was a natural and necessary sequence; for whatever be the moral condition of society, its most active elements will rise to the surface, and represent in an active form the more latent condition of the masses. Hence the maxim, "As are the rulers, so are the people." A wise and virtuous constituency would never produce corrupt representatives. The rulers are but the [conserved] forces of the people, rendered active and reflected back upon themselves; they are the forces which the people have originated and sustain. To the corruption of the representatives is due the corruption of public morals; *et vice versa*, the corruption of public morals sustains the corruption of the representatives.

THE DETERIORATION OF OUR IMMIGRANTS

Edward Bemis

Every one welcomes the skilled workingmen to our shores; but of the total immigration of about 1,837,000 males over fourteen years of age 1880–1886 inclusive, 53.3 per cent were merely unskilled day laborers. Of the total professional and skilled and unskilled immigrants from Italy in 1886, the per cent of unskilled was 60; from Austria, 67; from Hungary, 86; Ireland, 55; and England, 44. Only 36 per cent from Germany of the total skilled and unskilled workmen were unskilled, and from Scotland 27 per cent. In the above reckoning, farmers, who are comparatively unskilled, are classed among the skilled.

Professor Richmond M. Smith, the able Professor of Statistical Science at Columbia University, has recently shown in a public address the most significant fact of all in this matter of immigration, a fact which explains the present revulsion in public sentiment. He showed both that our own economic conditions in this country had changed so that we no longer had the need for unskilled labor as thirty years ago, and, what is even more important, that the character of our immigration has greatly changed for the worse within that time. That our present population of 56,000,000 is abundantly able from its own natural increase to supply all the demand hereafter for unskilled labor, especially now that our need for railroads has been so fully met, is self-evident. How about the deterioration of our immigrants?

European statistics show that the emigration from Ireland, which formerly came from the thrifty and intelligent of the North, comes now in far the largest measure from the poverty-stricken, illiterate counties of the west of the island. So in Germany. Emigration was at first and for a considerable period from the rich western provinces along the Rhine; now it is chiefly from the poorer population of Eastern Germany along the Polish and Austrian frontier.

Until recently there was hardly any immigration to us from Italy, Hungary, or Poland, which gives us our worst population. How is it

Edward Bemis, "Restriction of Immigration," *The Andover Review*, IX (March, 1888), 256–57.

now? Our entire immigration from all countries increased 162 per cent from the seven years preceding January 1, 1880, to the seven thereafter prior to 1887; but the Italian immigration, nearly all of which comes from Southern Italy, the most degraded portion, grew from 35,823 to 142,942, or a gain of 300 per cent, and has more than doubled the past year, jumping from 21,295 in 1886 to about 44,000 in 1887. Equally startling are the figures of our Hungarian immigration, which grew from 5,366 in 1873–1879 inclusive, to 62,593 in 1880–1886 inclusive, a gain of 1,016 per cent, or tenfold! The rapid increase still continues.

The causes are not far to seek, and have been pointed out by many. It is easier to come to this country now than twenty or forty years ago, and consequently poorer and less enterprising people can come. There is no longer a natural selection of the best, the most thrifty and ener-getic, when all can come.

source 6

The French-Canadian Immigrants

Carroll Wright

Carroll Wright, who was America's most eminent labor statistician of the late nineteenth century, wrote both selections. His remarks in the first selection occasioned a sharp rely from spokesmen for the French-Canadian immigrants, and the second extract presents a portion of Wright's reaction to their defense.

THE CHINESE OF THE EASTERN STATES

With some exceptions the Canadian French are the Chinese of the Eastern States. They care nothing for our institutions, civil, political, or educational. They do not come to make a home among us, to dwell with

Massachusetts Bureau of Labor Statistics, *Annual Report*, No. 12 (1881), 469–70.

us as citizens, and so become a part of us; but their purpose is merely
to sojourn a few years as aliens, touching us only at a single point, that
of work, and, when they have gathered out of us what will satisfy their
ends, to get them away to whence they came, and bestow it there. They
are a horde of industrial invaders, not a stream of stable settlers. Voting,
with all that it implies, they care nothing about. Rarely does one of them
become naturalized. They will not send their children to school if they
can help it, but endeavor to crowd them into the mills at the earliest
possible age. To do this they deceive about the age of their children
with brazen effrontery. They deceive also about their schooling, de-
claring that they have been to school the legal time, when they know
they have not, and do not intend that they shall. And when at length
they are cornered by the school officers, and there is no other escape,
often they scrabble together what few things they have, and move away
to some other place where they are unknown, and where they hope by
a repetition of the same deceits to escape the schools entirely, and keep
the children at work right on in the mills. And when, as is indeed sometimes the case, any of them are so situated that they cannot escape at
all, then the stolid indifference of the children wears out the teacher
with what seems to be an idle task.

These people have one good trait. They are indefatigable workers,
and docile. All they ask is to be set to work, and they care little who
rules them or how they are ruled. To earn all they can by no matter
how many hours of toil, to live in the most beggarly way so that out of
their earnings they may spend as little for living as possible, and to
carry out of the country what they can thus save: this is the aim of
the Canadian French in our factory districts. Incidentally they must
have some amusements; and, so far as the males are concerned, drinking and smoking and lounging constitute the sum of these.

Now, it is not strange that so sordid and low a people should awaken
corresponding feelings in the managers, and that these should feel that,
the longer the hours for such people, the better, and that to work them
to the uttermost is about the only good use they can be put to. Nor is
it strange that this impression is so strong, that the managers overlook
for the time being all the rest of the operatives, and think that every
thing should be shaped to these lowest ones. Yet the same principle
which we have stated as showing the right way of conduct in the former
case should direct here also. Society should be shaped to the better

portion of the people; and where the case requires it the laws should be so amended and enforced that these people will either be coerced to conform to our established ways, or else go where the already established ways of the country do please them.

A REVISED OPINION

. . . We have taken pains to learn if any malice existed in the minds of the informants of the Bureau against the French, and are perfectly satisfied that no malice entered into the case; our informants thought, and still think, they were speaking the truth generally, but freely admit that their statements were too sweeping. It is evident, however, that some prejudice existed in their minds, for they but echoed the impressions existing in the minds of the people; and these impressions were the legitimate results of the policy and actions of certain classes of the French, as will be seen, but which were allowed to apply to the race.

The reports made to the Bureau came from localities where the French Canadians are not well organized, where they too often live in a way that subjects them to severe criticisms, and where, from a variety of causes, they have been accustomed to change their residence with a frequency which usually led people to think of them as a roving race. It has been with them as with all peoples of strongly marked characteristics: the worst and lowest specimens have been taken as representatives of the race.

:•   •.   •

Now, while it would have been very easy to have combated the evidence given at the hearing, and to have introduced much testimony to support the statements contained in the report of last year, and while we see no reason to strike out the statements therein made when read in the light of the present report, it is very gratifying to know that a wide and rapidly growing movement has arisen among the French Canadians within the past few years, towards becoming citizens, fully

Massachusetts Bureau of Labor Statistics, *Annual Report*, No. 13 (1882), 88–89, 91–92.

identified with us as a permanent and honorable part of our people; and in their every endeavor in this direction Americans can but wish them God-speed. Partly as a result of this movement efforts for repatriation have been abandoned, and it is now the settled policy of the Canadian French, who come among us, to come as permanent residents, and to be Americans. Although this movement is recent, yet it is accompanied by such laudable endeavors to acquire a knowledge of our institutions, and to take active and intelligent part in our national life, that doubtless our best wishes concerning them will be realized.

source 7

When the Breaker Starts Up Full-Time

Among immigrant groups, hostility toward each other was often as marked as any prejudice by native-born Americans against newcomers. This ballad was written in the 1880's. It was sung to the tune of "My Pearl is a Bowery Girl." The first stanza and chorus have been omitted.

I'll ne'er stick me fist in a washtub,
The Chinee man he'll have me trade,
I'll ne'er pick a coal off the dirt bank;
I'll buy everything ready-made.
We'll dress up our children like fairies,
We'll build up a house big and fine,
And we'll move away from the Hungaries—
When the breaker starts up full-time.

The Hungaries won't work with me, Paddy;
They say too much no good his place.
They always lose time after pay-day,
Its meself sure that ne'er liked that race.

George Korson (Compiler), *Songs and Ballads of the Anthracite Miner* (New York, 1926), pp. 44–45.

> They won't load their cairs off the livil,
> They want runnin' chutes, do ye mind?
> But we'll chase thim away to the divil—
> When the breaker starts up full-time.

source 8

The Condition of the Millworkers

Elizabeth Buffum Chase

> Elizabeth Buffum Chase had been an active abolitionist and a
> leader of the anti-slavery forces in Rhode Island. She was also inter-
> ested in women's rights, including suffrage, conditions of labor for
> women and children, and the treatment of women and children in
> penal institutions. Note her emphasis upon environmental influences,
> rather than inherent ethnic characteristics, as the reason for the poor
> situation in which the immigrants found themselves.

Thus it is a fact, that a very large number of women and girls,
from ten years old to forty or fifty, are employed in the cotton and
woolen mills of the northern and middle states of this country, mostly
in New England. It is, therefore, a subject of grave concern as to what
is their actual condition, and, what are the duties of other women
toward them. Many of those born in England, Ireland, and Canada
cannot read or write; and of those who have had a chance in our public
schools, most of them have gone to work so early, that their schooling
has been of the most rudimentary character, and is easily forgotten.
They are excluded from the society of their own sex outside of the
factory by a variety of barriers—chief of which are their foreign birth
or extraction, *their poverty,* their want of education, and the necessity
that they should be always at work. Two other causes also contribute
largely to this exclusion. These people are mostly Catholic in their

Labor Standard (Fall River) (December 10, 1881), 1; (December 31,
1881), 1.

religion, and this excludes them from Protestant companionship, and the other is, the growing tendency in our civilization toward class distinctions.

Many of these operatives live a floating life. Unsettled from their native homes, the older members of the families never become truly nationalized anywhere; and the children grow up with the idea that they are an alien people. So, trifling circumstances, and the hope of improving their condition, lead them to move about, and thus they continue unthrifty and poor; and whatever unfortunate results follow, they all bear with most hardship upon the women. On the contrary, those who remain in one place, if they cultivate habits of industry and sobriety, do constantly improve their circumstances, and become more and more assimilated to the native inhabitants. But, with rare exceptions, they have brought with them the inherited improvidence, which comes from many generations in hopeless poverty, under old world oppression.

•   •   •

The ascent from ignorance, poverty, coarseness and hardship, to culture, wealth, refinement and ease, is by slow steps of progress, and those at the highest point are fortunate in having had the way opened for them by others who have preceded them. And surely it is their duty to hold out to those behind them a helping hand, in order to lift them as far as possible to a level with themselves.

Immigrant Labor in the Clothing Industry

Illinois Bureau of Labor Statistics

The Biennial Report of 1892 included an investigation of the employment of immigrant labor in the clothing industry. Much of this work was carried on at piece rates in the home of the worker. Unlike many reports by state bureaus of labor statistics in this period, this one was based upon personal visits to the home of the worker by the investigator, and not upon the fragmentary and unchecked evidence gleaned from questionnaires mailed to selected workingmen. (See Source 10.) The conditions described in this selection were repeated in other urban areas.

Vest maker.—Norwegian woman aged 43; in this country 3 years; speaks no English; lives with an older brother, who presses and stitches; the two can make 3 vests in a day, at 75 cents to $1.25 apiece; rarely get work enough and the woman does washing in the intervals.

Vest finisher.—Swedish woman of 50, finishes vests at 10 and 12 cents per dozen; in 6 months earned $57.08; 5 years in America, but speaks no English; complains that the [employer] does not pay until 30 days after delivery of goods, and then not in full.

Vest finisher.—Polish woman of 60, husband superannuated, finishes vests at 1 cent apiece; earned 64 cents in one week; has no book, but thinks she earned $50 or $60 in 5 months; 11 years in America; speaks no English; takes 4 adult male boarders, and with her sewing supports her husband.

Trousers finisher.—Polish woman, 6 years in this country, speaks no English, 26 years old, husband a laborer, gets 6 cents a pair for finishing trousers, and finishes 6 pairs a day.

Hand-finisher.—Polish woman of 30, two months in America, has earned $3 finishing trousers at 5½ cents a pair. Speaks no English; has

Illinois Bureau of Labor Statistics, *Biennial Report,* No. 7 (1892), pp. 404–5.

never attended school; husband is a laborer. They have seven children; an uncle and a grandmother live with them and contribute to the support of the family. They occupy 4 rooms in a bad neighborhood and their home conditions are wretched.

Hand-finisher.—Polish woman 50 years old, widow, two months in America, has earned $3 finishing trousers at 5½ cents apiece; has never attended school; with the assistance of three others she supports a family of eleven persons. They all live in 4 rooms, for which a monthly rental of $7 is paid.

Hand-finisher.—German Polish woman, 35 years old, finishes trousers at 7 and 8 cents a pair. Earns 42 cents a day regularly; has been 11 years in America, but speaks no English. Never attended school; began regular work at the age of 30, and lives at home with her father, who is a stonemason, and owns his house of 5 rooms.

Hand-finisher.—Russian Polish woman aged 25, has been in America one year, speaks no English, and has never attended school. Finishes trousers at 5 cents a pair; carries her work one mile and finishes 6 pairs a day. Has worked regularly 6 months. Husband is a woodturner; they have two small children and occupy three rooms, for which they pay a monthly rental of $5.

Hand-finisher.—Prussian woman of 27; finishes trousers at 5½ cents a pair; can finish from 6 to 8 pairs a day; earned $5.28 in 16 days; in America 18 months but speaks no English. Never attended school; husband is a brick layer. They have one child, and pay $5 a month rent for 3 rooms.

Hand-finisher.—German Polish woman 35 years old who has never attended school. Finishes trousers at 7 cents a pair; earns 42 cents a day regularly; has worked 5 years. Husband is a stone-mason, family consists of 7 persons, four of whom contribute to the general support. They occupy 5 rooms in a bad neighborhood, for which they pay $7 per month.

Trousers makers.—This Russian family of father, mother and 6 children live in three rooms on the second floor of a rear tenement. The father, mother, two daughters and a cousin work together making trousers at 65 cents a dozen pairs. They do not know the name or address of their employer. A man brings a wagon load of trousers, and when they are finished calls for them. They work 7 days a week; the number of hours per day depends upon the supply of trousers; they often work 16 and 18 hours and make 7 and 7½ dozen pairs in a day. There are three machines, the mother finishes, and the cousin is a presser and button-hole maker. The contractor absconded owing them $40, which they in turn owe for rent and food. They are now working for another contractor, at 35 cents per dozen pairs. Their destitution is very great; the mother's health is delicate, as is also that of the daughters; neither have ever attended school; the younger children attend the school of the United Hebrew Charities.

Machine-hand.—Russian girl aged 17 years, has worked 4 days making knee-pants, has been in America two weeks and is working for nothing to learn the trade; has never attended school; speaks only jargon.

Machine-hands.—Two Russian girls 16 and 17 years old; have worked regularly for three years, stitching knee-pants at from 6 to 10 cents per dozen pairs. They work 10 hours and stitch three dozen pairs a day. They rent two machines, for which they pay $1.50 a week. The family of four occupy 4 dark rooms on the ground floor of a wretched tenement. The girls support their mother. Their brother, who is a teacher of Hebrew, pays their rent. They have attended school in Russia and have learned to read, write and speak English.

Hand-finishers.—Italian woman and three daughters who finish knee-pants at 8 cents a dozen pairs. By working steadily they can altogether finish 8 dozen in a day. They do not know the name or address of their employer. They live in filth in the basement of a rear tenement; they speak no English; none of them have ever attended school; the father is a sewer digger; the mother is 36 and the daughters 14, 15 and 16 years of age.

Hand-finishers.—Two Italian families live together in three small rooms; each family pays half the rent, the total amount being $7 per month. The two husbands are fruit peddlers. The wives work together finishing knee-pants at 7 cents per dozen pairs; they finish 5 dozen pairs a day. They are each aged 26 years; have never attended school, speak no English. In this house a man has just recovered from an attack of malignant diphtheria, without having interfered with the work of finishing knee-pants in this room nor the one above.

Hand-finisher.—Italian woman 33 years old. Just commenced to work on knee-pants, at 6 cents a dozen pairs. In America 3 years but speaks no English; has never attended school; husband is a street sweeper; they occupy 4 rooms jointly with 3 other families, each paying

$2.50 of the $10 per month charged for rent. The entire number occupying these 4 rooms are 9 grown persons and 9 children. The men work
in the country and come home twice a month, on alternate Saturdays.

source 10

Living Conditions of Immigrant Families

Illinois Bureau of Labor Statistics

Inadequate financing, uneven administration, and political pressures
marked the operation of the state bureaus of labor statistics in this
period. Employers, labor unions and individual workers were often
uncooperative, and the published reports of the bureaus were frequently filled with unanalyzed and unrepresentative data. The type
of documentary evidence found in this selection, as in Source 9, is
less suspect since these Reports describe the results of personal visits
by the Bureau's investigators. One cannot exclude misinformation in
these capsule remarks since workers usually kept poor records and
were often suspicious, if not uncooperative. Thus much was left to
the judgment of the investigator, who might be quite unsympathetic
to the habits and attitudes of these workers. However, this survey
is valuable in suggesting the living conditions of workingmen, the
importance of child labor, and the variety of situations within a
group that might otherwise be lumped together quantitatively.

No. 36.	LABORER	*Bohemian.*

EARNINGS—
Of father .... $ 480
Of son, aged twenty-three 384
Of son, aged seventeen 250
        Total $1,114

Illinois Bureau of Labor Statistics, *Biennial Report*, No. 3 (1884), pp.
370–71.

CONDITION—Family numbers 6—parents and four boys, aged twenty-three, seventeen, fourteen and twelve. Father works 52 weeks per year; owns comfortable house of 4 rooms. The boys help support the family. House is comfortably furnished. Their expenditures equal their income.

FOOD—*Breakfast*—Bread, butter and coffee.
    Dinner—Lunches.
    Supper—Meat, vegetables, bread and coffee.

COST OF LIVING—

Fuel	$ 30
Meat and groceries	600
Clothing	150
Boots and shoes	20
Dry goods	30
Books, papers, etc.	20
Trades unions	11
Sundries	253
Total	$1,114

No. 38.   LABORER   *Scandinavian.*

EARNINGS—

Of father	$320
Of wife	100
Total	$420

CONDITION—Family numbers 8—parents and six children, four girls, twins three months, one two and one three years, two boys, one five and the other seven. Live in a house containing 4 rooms, and pay $11 per month rent. House very poorly furnished, and a miserable affair altogether.

FOOD—*Breakfast*—Bread, meat and coffee.
    Dinner—Bread, vegetables and coffee.
    Supper—Bread and coffee, etc.

COST OF LIVING—

Rent	$132
Fuel	33
Meat and groceries	165
Clothing, boots and shoes and dry goods	65
Sundries	25
Total	$420

No. 39   LABORER.   *Scandinavian.*

EARNINGS—
Of father $405
Of son, aged eleven 200
Total $605

CONDITION—Family numbers 5—parents and three children, two boys aged nine and eleven, and one girl seven. Live in a rented house, containing 4 rooms, for which $8 per month is paid. House is a frame structure, poorly furnished with no carpets. They overrun their income.

FOOD—*Breakfast*—Bread, butter, meat and coffee.
        Dinner—Bread, meat and vegetables.
        Supper—Bread, butter, meat and tea.

COST OF LIVING—
Rent .... $ 96
Fuel 30
Meat 200
Groceries 225
Clothing 30
Boots and shoes 20
Dry goods 25
Books, papers, etc. 3
Sundries 3
Total $632

Progress and Its Discontents

Josiah Strong

> Strong was one of the more influential Protestant clergymen who
> sought to apply Christian values to economic and social problems.
> He also advocated the supremacy of the Anglo-Saxon race, and thus
> opposed unrestricted immigration.

The average workingman two or three generations ago would no
doubt have been well content with the hours, wages, food, lodgings, and
clothes of the average workingman today, but during the nineteenth
century public schools, public libraries, art galleries, museums, exposi-
tions, public parks, newspapers, and travel have all become common.
Advertising, which is the art of making people want things, appeals to
all classes alike. There has been a wonderful leveling up of the "common" people. Once great men were gods, and slaves were less than
human. Now all alike are *men,* having much the same wants and quite
the same rights. The spread of democracy, the growth of individualism,
the equality of all men before the law have suggested the idea of equality of condition and made the masses feel that they are as capable of
enjoying the good things of life as the classes. All these have contributed powerfully to increase the intelligence and wants of workingmen,
and the resulting elevation of the standard of living has made a home,
a table, a coat seem almost intolerable which once would have been
deemed comfortable and even luxurious. The workingman of today may
have, if you please, twice as much as his grandfather had, but he knows,
say, ten times as much and wants ten times as much; hence his discontent.

• • •

Josiah Strong, *The New Era* (New York: The Baker and Taylor Co., 1893),
pp. 141, 147–49.

The spirit of American civilization is eminently progressive. The increase of our population, the springing up of new cities and the growth of old ones, the extension of our railway and telegraph systems, the increase of our agricultural, manufacturing and mining products, the development of our natural resources, the accumulation of our national wealth—all these are simply enormous. Such are the progress of invention and the increase of knowledge, and such is the rapidity with which important changes jostle each other, that years seem like generations.

In the midst of all this progress, the workingman feels that he is practically standing still or worse. He sees many belonging to other classes waxing rich, while he is perhaps unable to support his family. If he could feed and fatten himself and his family on the east wind and lay by all his wages, it would take a lifetime to save as much as many business and professional men make in a single year.

His wants are increasing with his intelligence, but there is no corresponding increase of his means. We hear it often said and often denied that while the rich are growing richer the poor are growing poorer. The poor are not poorer in the sense that their wages will buy less of the necessaries of life or that they are rated lower on the tax list, but it is true in the sense that there is a greater disparity now between the workingman's income and his wants than ever before, and that is the only sense worth considering in this connection.

Now here is the point of my contention: the question whether the condition of the workingman has *materially* improved in this century is stoutly debated, *but the question whether there has been most wonderful material progress in general is not debatable;* no one doubts it. Evidently, then, the progress of the workingman is not proportionate to the general material progress. And this fact gives him just ground for complaint.

The Universality of the Success Ethic

THE ASPIRATIONS OF THE WORKINGMAN

Henry W. Cherouny

This selection originally appeared in an article written in 1888. Cherouny was a master printer who had been influenced by the social gospel. He believed that the universality of the success ethic was a sign of weakness in American society.

Industrial giants impelling incessant speculation create a restlessness and haste among the skilled and unskilled masses of laborers that drive them in search of chances from town to town. Senseless competition keeps them in a state of constant migration from place to place, from street to street, from house to house. The sturdy artisans and poor day-laborers, the small tradesmen and mechanics, those having a little capital as well as those living on credit, all must follow the mysterious beck of the industrial magnates. The small householders fly hither and thither, where new hopes or better prospects brighten the horizon, or where there are grocers and butchers who do not know how much the newcomers owe in other quarters. Each business misfortune compels a change of residence, each promise of triflingly higher wages, as well as each reduction of income, creates a shiftiness and nervousness which cannot allow a thought of the common affairs to arise. There is either a general stagnation of business, which is to the industrial population like a whirlwind, scattering neighbors and separating too often fathers, mothers and children, while the cherished household goods go to the auction room or pawnbroker. Or there is a rush of business during which all make money and spend it foolishly. Why should the poor care? The next cloud is already rising in Wall Street. It will surely burst, and the

Henry W. Cherouny, *The Burial of the Apprentice: A True Story from Life in a Union Workshop* (New York: Cherouny Printing and Publishing, 1900), pp. 68–69.

little savings of the laborers will certainly disappear in the torrent about to sweep through the industrial world. Be happy, then, while the sun shines, drink and smoke, sing and dance, and curse the long-faced Yankee who talks of virtue and temperance.

The people hope for good luck; this of course means easy acquisition of money. The world teaches them that money is the *summum bonum*. All hunt for it, and by what means it is acquired is immaterial. Now, as the passion goes they gamble in lotteries, or, if they can, in Wall Street. To-morrow they invest their whole possessions in spurious stocks or risky business undertakings. If prosperity shines they indulge in vulgar luxury. The porter imitates the boss, the servant outshines the lady. Superstition and credulity increase, and humbug prospers. And, when misfortune overtakes them, they allow themselves to be helped along by Christian charity.

WHO IS A BANKER?

Terence V. Powderly

> The Knights of Labor barred bankers from membership, for they were clearly not part of labor. But as Powderly's confused effort here indicates, it was difficult in America to determine just who was a "banker."

"A person owning bank stock and deriving profits therefrom" is not, according to the popular acceptation of the term, a banker; but if a man owns sufficient bank stock to enable him to dictate who shall officer the bank, he certainly is a banker. If he does not own enough for that, and has a desire to own it, then we must judge him by his desire. If we judge him by that standard we would discover that nearly every man in the Order would be a banker. But it cannot be the desire that makes a banker of a man; it must be his interest in a bank. It occurs to me that a man having an interest in a bank is, to a certain extent, a banker. The man who holds bank stock has an interest in the bank. By going back a little further we find that the man who deposits

Knights of Labor, *Decisions of the General Master Workman, Revised and Codified* (Philadelphia, 1887), p. 34.

in a bank has an interest in the same, and his interest is exactly the same as the president of the bank, viz.: to make all he can of his money. We must draw the line somewhere, else we will all be bankers; therefore we must carefully observe the uses a man makes of his investment and judge him accordingly. I cannot decide that a man holding bank stock is unfit for membership until I hear something regarding his character. That a man has money enough to invest in bank stock or government bonds does not debar him from membership, for poverty is not the chief qualification required of a member.

source **13**

The Success Ethic Endangers Unionism

The Furniture Workers' Union was socialist in outlook while the Pattern Makers' League was a conservative craft union. Although they viewed trade unionism from quite different political positions, both organizations were aware that the American worker was attracted to the success ethic, and both recognized the danger of this attitude for their cause.

THE CAPITALISTIC SPIRIT AND THE WORKINGMAN

Furniture Workers' Union of North America

The natural and justifiable longing of every person for wellbeing and independence has, among many workingmen, been developed in a wrong direction. They imitate the so-called higher classes in the maxim "Everyone for himself and God for us all." Yet they do not imitate them in combining for a common interest of their class. They lose sight of the fact that all laborers of whichever complexion, religion or political conviction, are equally fleeced, and that their isolation for

Furniture Workers' Union of North America, Central Committee, *Normal Workday of Eight Hours* (New York, 1879), pp. 1–2.

particular interests is always to their disadvantage, their common organization always to their advantage. . . .

Through the unexampled prosperity of American industry and
commerce after the Civil War which lasted for half a decade, the
working people learned to think and act in a capitalistic way. The
demand for workingmen and their organizations had raised wages to
20 or 30 dollars a week or more. In their prosperity the workingmen
forgot that employers pay high wages only when they cannot help it.
The furniture and piano workers neglected their organizations, and
overworked themselves in such a manner that the demand for their
work was diminished, and wages were reduced to a more modest scale.
There was no lack of farseeing leaders in these decades who admonished
their fellows to stick to their organizations to which they owed so much.
But the capitalistic spirit of society had taken hold of the masses, and
the voice of the leaders was disregarded.

The workingmen were striving to deposit as much money as possible in the savings banks, to insure their lives at the rate of thousands
of dollars, to buy tenement houses or to become members of a building
society. For such purposes hard work was necessary; all imaginable
shifts in the manner of working had to be invented.

ONLY ORGANIZED LABOR COMMANDS THE RESPECT
OF THE EMPLOYER

Pattern Makers' National League of America

Pattern makers should be, by reason of the many advantages they
possess over other trades, the best remunerated and enjoy the best conditions in the industrial world. Compared with other trades that are
receiving higher wages, shorter hours, and all that goes to make up the
sum total of earthly happiness, the Pattern Maker should be among
the highest paid mechanics. His trade is one that requires the highest
grade of mechanical skill, and takes years of careful study and practice
to master its intricacies. Yet we find many of the occupations requiring
far less of mechanical knowledge and experience receiving much higher

Pattern Makers' National League of America, *Monthly Journal,* V (September, 1896), 2–3.

wages. Why this is so can be easily explained. It is lack of thorough organization. The best paid of the trades are those that are best organized. The greatest obstacle to the thorough organization of the Pattern Makers has been a sort of vain conceit on the part of the great majority of our trade that their individual merit or abilities as mechanics would always command for them the best of everything in this world. And so they have for years gone on hugging this fond delusion to their souls, and their wages have steadily decreased, their ranks have been invaded by interlopers from other wood-working trades, and in most instances, except where they have been progressive enough to organize, their conditions are not much better than that of the common laborer. Is it not time that our fellow-craftsmen begin to realize that as individuals they cannot cope with the great combinations of capital that control every avenue of industry; that the individual worker is only regarded as a part of the productive machine, that can be replaced or duplicated at any time; that no consideration of personal worth or merit ever enters into the ethics of modern business practice. It is only the organized that can command the respect of the organized. Organized capital vs. organized labor are the only forces that have any influence upon the industrial welfare of the country. Each has a wholesome respect for the other. They have measured strength, have crossed swords, and by so doing have learned that each is entitled to consideration.

source 14

The Increased Difficulty of Starting in Business

Joseph Finnerty

> This congressional investigation produced a rich store of testimony about the position of the worker. The selection is from the remarks made by Joseph Finnerty, a member of the brass workers' union. His observations typify the complaints of labor leaders during the 1880's about the deteriorating condition of the artisan.

IMPOSSIBILITY OF SAVING FROM PRESENT WAGES

Q. Do the bronze workers who are married men lay up anything, as a general rule?—A. No, sir; they do not. If they happen to be able to make both ends meet at the end of the year they are doing wonders. Of course in every class of people there may be one or two in a hundred that would get rich, no matter what wages they received, but the bronze worker generally saves no money, and if he can keep his family in food and clothes and pay his rent he feels that he is doing wonders.

Q. Before the introduction of this machinery, by which the man has been reduced to being one-tenth or one-fourth of a complete tradesman, how much capital did it take to become a brass worker on one's own account?

INCREASED DIFFICULTY OF STARTING IN BUSINESS

A. At that time a man that had $300 or $400 could start a brass shop himself and make a living out of it, but to-day no man who understands the condition of the trade would start with less than $5,000. He

United States Senate, Education and Labor Committee, *Report Upon the Relations between Labor and Capital,* Vol. I (Washington, D.C.: Government Printing Office, 1885), pp. 744–45.

would need that much to supply machinery and start his shop, and then he would have a hard road to travel.

Q. At that time, if a man had a room large enough to work in, and had his tools and a little money to buy the raw material, he could become an independent workman, you say, making his brass work himself and selling it to the public?—A. Yes, sir.

*   *   *

Q. Fourteen years ago, as I understand you, a brass worker might hope, by prudence and economy, to become an independent worker for himself?—A. Yes, sir; but now the trade is controlled by the larger companies. They have their drummers or agents in different parts of the country, and it takes capital to carry on the business in that way; and in order to establish an independent brass shop you have to have your connections made all through the country, something which a poor man cannot do.

Q. So you consider that it is about hopeless for a brass worker now to aspire to the condition of brass manufacturer?—A. Yes, sir; it is hopeless, and I think they will not try it any more.

*   *   *

Q. . . . Has the stimulus, the inducement to save by close living, and all that sort of thing been lessened in any degree by the fact that there is now no hope of a workman ever becoming a boss or having an independent establishment of his own?—A. All the brass worker cares about now is to hold his job, and he will put up with any kind of abuse as long as he is not discharged.

Q. But fourteen years ago you say it was different.—A. Yes, sir. He would not stand any abuse at all then, and no abuse would be offered to him then; he was treated as a skilled workman.

Q. Did many of the workers in brass fourteen years ago actually get into the position of independent brass manufacturers?—A. Oh, yes, sir. There are some of our leading firms to-day that started under the different condition that existed fourteen or fifteen years ago.

Q. Were these men more provident or economical or stingy at that time, as a rule, than the workmen are now, when they have no hope of

becoming independent workers?—A. The men who are bosses now, and
who were workmen at that time, were not saving or stingy, and while
they were merely getting journeymen's wages they did not save anything; but when they got to be foremen, then they commenced to save,
and when they became superintendents they made enough money to
start for themselves.

source 15

The Ambition of All Trainmen

> The attitude of "Jack Rabbit" in this selection represented the feel-
> ings of many skilled workers who turned their sights on promotion
> or some other form of entry into the middle class. This created
> problems for the trade unions, and it was a factor in the failure of
> the socialists to convert a significant number of American workers.

EDITOR RAILWAY CONDUCTOR:

Admitting the success of the Order of Railway Conductors, and
giving that organization credit for all it has accomplished in the past,
in the full meaning of its motto, Justice, Charity and Fidelity, the question that now confronts its members is how can such an organization
be made to fit its members to occupy higher positions in railway service?
There is a large field yet uncultivated by the members of the Order,
and when properly cultivated they should reap an abundant harvest.
The ambition of all trainmen is promotion to the position of conductor.
So far so good, but don't let your ambition stop there. Keep on, and by
strict attention to your duties as conductor, show your fitness to occupy
such position as yardmaster and trainmaster, which are steps to the
position of division and general superintendents. Methinks I hear some
Brothers say when they read this, "Jack Rabbit, your aspirations are too
high. The chances for the promotion of a conductor to the offices named
are not to be thought of." Brothers, you are mistaken; there should not
be an office herein named, to which a successful conductor may not

The Railway Conductor, XIII (February 1896), 129–30.

aspire. The railway companies have given us encouragement for higher aspirations, by setting a standard. They say to all who make application for train service. What is your penmanship? Are you a fair speller? Are you fair in arithmetic? And what is your ability in composing a letter? Last but not least, do you drink or gamble? All of which I approve. We now have the rough material to work on; what is going to be the outcome of the finished article? Why, a better show for promotion than we veterans have had in the past. The young men who are now ready to step in and fill the places of men who are too old to continue in the service will need no second invitation to become members of our organization if we commence to elevate and fit our members to occupy these higher positions. There will then be an object for them to affiliate with our Order.

.   .   .

Come, Brothers, let us set the ball to rolling and hang out our sign and write thereon, "We, the members of the Order of Railway Conductors, are in the market to furnish practical freight and passenger conductors, yardmasters, trainmasters, division and general superintendents." We have a trademark that will carry with it a guarantee, and is emblematic of our organization, O. R. C.

Terre Haute, Ind.   JACK RABBIT.

Machines of Almost Superhuman Ingenuity

Charles Litchman

> We have already noted the desire of the skilled worker to retain his
> distinctive skill, which was the basis of his dignity as a worker and
> his means of entry into the middle class. In this selection, Charles
> Litchman—a Grand Secretary of the Knights of Labor, a leader in
> the Knights of St. Crispin, which sought to organize shoemakers
> in the late 1860's and early 1870's, and a firm believer in producers'
> and consumers' cooperatives—indicates some of the effects of ma-
> chinery which seemed to threaten the livelihood and security of the
> skilled worker. Note also that Litchman recognized the gains that
> machinery might ultimately provide.

. . . The first effect of the introduction of labor-saving machinery
is the degradation of labor.

THE CHAIRMAN. How?

MR. LITCHMAN. By the subdivision of labor a man now is no longer
a tradesman. He is a part of a tradesman. In my own trade of shoemaking, twenty years ago the work was done almost entirely by hand,
and the man had to learn how to make a shoe. Now, with the use of
machines of almost superhuman ingenuity, a man is no longer a shoemaker, but only the sixty-fourth part of a shoemaker, because there are
sixty-four subdivisions in making shoes; and a man may work forty
years at our trade, and at the end of forty years he will know no more
about making a whole shoe than when he commenced business.

THE CHAIRMAN. He would only know how to make a peg or a
waxed-end?

MR. LITCHMAN. Yes; or he would be a laster, or a beveler, or heeler,
or nailer, or he would be running and using a machine, or a peg-measure,

United States House of Representatives, *Investigation by a Select Committee
of The House of Representatives Relative to the Causes of the General Depression in Labor and Business; and as to Chinese Immigration* (Washington, D.C.: Government Printing Office, 1879), pp. 429–32.

or attending to any one of the 64 subdivisions into which the trade is parceled out. It takes 64 men now to make a shoe by machinery. There you see is an element that comes into the labor question which is very important, and which is at the same time more difficult to handle. You cannot turn back the hands upon the dial of human progress and say that all machinery must be banished. You would not take up the rails, destroy the locomotive, and break up the railroad cars, and go back to the stage-coaches and horses. You would not tear down the telegraph poles, break up telegraph instruments, and destroy the cables that run under the ocean. Yet all these improvements, while in the abstract they benefit mankind, have had as their first result the degradation of labor by the subdivision of labor. Under our present wage-labor system, capital gets the whole advantage of the introduction of human brain into human labor.

THE CHAIRMAN. The consumer gets some of the advantages.

MR. LITCHMAN. The consumer gets some indirectly. That is where the abstract benefit comes in. I admit all that. I admit that the shoe which formerly cost $7 can now be bought at $3, but one shoe of former times would outwear two pairs of shoes now; so that it is pretty nearly the same. . . .

•   •   •

I am now going to speak of one thing in regard to the effect of labor-saving machinery to show you how great the problem is which we have under consideration. It does not take a manufacturer very long to understand that a certain piece of machinery can be run just as well by a child as by a man. Then boys and girls are employed at it and the husband and father is set adrift to join the grand army of tramps who move up and down the land. The child is employed at this work because he can be employed at a child's wages. Every child thus employed takes the place of a man, and a man is removed from work in order to make room for the child. Thus we not only destroy the labor of the present generation, but in the natural order of things, when these boys and girls become the fathers and mothers of a new generation, we have made a draft upon the future which will be honored with compound interest. If you go into the mills of this State [Massachusetts] (and God knows I would say nothing against my own native State, for I have all the pride of State that any man has) you will find children employed that are scarcely four feet high, who are just literally coining their young hearts' blood into dollars and cents.

∙ ∙ ∙

. . . It may be asked how we are going to remedy this matter of the introduction of machinery. I would first enforce all labor laws, and through their influence I would compel the attendance of children at the public schools. That would of necessity, under the laws of this State, give twenty weeks' schooling every year to every boy and girl in the State. Then I would encourage by all possible just legislation the forming of co-operative associations, manufacturing, distributive, and mercantile. I would in every way give encouragement to the ownership of homes by working men. And pardon me for saying right here, that if I had been in Congress, I would have given all the support in my power to the homestead bill of Mr. Wright. Another means of meeting the introduction of labor saving machinery is by reducing the hours of labor. It is claimed that a reduction of the hours of labor means a reduction of the wages paid to labor, but history proves the contrary. The workingmen of Massachusetts earn more now that they only work eleven hours a day, than they did when they worked fifteen hours a day. . . .

∙ ∙ ∙

. . . [I]f under the old system of doing things it required a certain number of hours to do a certain amount of work, and if through the introduction of machinery that same amount of work can be done in half the time that it formerly required, it seems to me that there is no excuse for working men the same length of time that they formerly worked, because the inevitable result of doing so would be to throw half the number of men out of employment. In my own trade, the introduction of machinery has reduced the number of shoemakers in this State from 70,000 to 50,000. So that I say we can meet the introduction of labor-saving machinery first and above all by co-operation, whereby labor can own a portion of the machinery, and second by reducing the hours of labor. As a proof of that, shoemaking in this State used to occupy about eleven months in the year. Now it occupies only eight months at the farthest, and in some instances only seven months, so that the men are idle from four to five months in the year.

THE CHAIRMAN. What causes that?

MR. LITCHMAN. Because in seven months they can produce enough to last for the year by machinery. If you decrease the hours of labor, then you have got either to increase the number of machines or the number of men. If you increase the number of machines, you give employment to somebody to make the machines, so that the thing will even up. Now if all the work of mankind can be done by machinery, mankind should have the advantage of it. Here is a radical point which I propose to put in. I believe that the time will come when mankind will have two Sundays in the week instead of one—one of them to devote to himself, and the other to devote to his God. He will have five days for labor and two days for rest. That may appear radical and theoretical, and all that, but I think it is perfectly logical.

source 17

Unity Among Workingmen

John Swinton

John Swinton was active in the cause of labor reform during the last third of the century, and in 1883 he began to edit and publish his own weekly labor newspaper which appeared until 1887. During this brief period, it provoked controversy, produced excellent articles and commentary, and, in its failure, illustrated the perennial problem of the labor press of this era—the lack of support from workers themselves. Swinton had originally been trained as a printer, but from 1860 until his death in 1901, he was a journalist and author. This selection indicates the very real conflict that existed within organized labor between the theoretical desirability of unity among workingmen, and the reality of an increasing conflict of interest between the skilled and unskilled.

John Swinton's Paper (October 3, 1886), 2.

To the Editor—

I notice that toward the approach of every full moon the editor of *Carpentry and Building* (a journal of New York City supposed to be devoted to the Building Trades) has to ventilate his brain in predicting the speedy annihilation of the K. of L. [Knights of Labor]. . . .

He also says that the "mechanic and unskilled laborer have no interests in common, and whatever is gained by unskilled labor is at the expense of skilled labor." I beg to differ with him on this point. When unskilled laborers are poorly paid we see many of them crowding into the ranks of skilled labor. Take, for instance, the carpenter trade. We find over one-third of the men almost entirely uneducated. Go back to the time when they bought their first hand saw and axe prior to entering the trade as carpenters; we find them employed as farm laborers, pick and shovel men, mill operatives, etc. Owing to the depression of, and low wages in, their several occupations, they are compelled, in order to maintain existence, to enter the ranks of skilled labor, much to the detriment of the same, for the prosperity of skilled labor depends upon the demand for it. Unskilled labor should be properly paid, for upon it depends largely the consumption and utilization of the products of skilled labor. The unskilled laborer is a necessity, and why has he not a right to improve his conditions as well as a skilled laborer.

I am a mechanic who served my time in learning a trade, yet I am not so ignorant or conceited as to say that men who are not up to the standard of my profession have not the same right to existence and to protection as I have.

I cannot see how any man born with the remotest spark of intelligence could make such assertions as does this editor. I am sure his views are not in keeping with the objects of the *Carpentry and Building* and give offense to many of its readers.

A Believer in Equity

The Inutility of Strikes

Locomotive Engineers' Monthly Journal

The Engineers coupled their belief in a mutuality of interest between workingmen and employers with strong opposition to strikes. This type of approach rapidly lost its support within organized labor as unions increasingly accepted the fixed position of the worker.

The labor question is one of present and permanent interest. The relations of employer and employed, of those who do the hard work and those who guide the great operations of numbers of people, and supply the money, without which those operations cannot be conducted—these are matters lying at the very root of social organization, and upon their adjustment depend the success or failure and the happiness or misery of society. And, however fanatics or demagogues may endeavor to disguise the truth, the interests of both classes are identical. The capitalist and the laborer are necessary to each other. The prosperity of the one is contingent with the prosperity of the other. When their respective interests, instead of going harmoniously forward, are permitted to come into collision, the result is sure to be damaging and may be disastrous to both. The wages of workingmen should not only be sufficient for their support—they should be as liberal as the conditions of trade or manufacture will allow. At the same time the fair profit of the capitalist must be considered, because unless a reasonable return for his investment be secured, the successful continuance of the business in which his men are engaged is impossible. On the one hand, the employer who pursues a niggardly policy toward workingmen, keeping them as nearly as possible at starvation wages, need not expect from them good and productive work. On the other hand, the intelligent working man must concede that, unless the interests of his employer as well as his own are regarded, the partnership cannot be advantageously maintained. For they are really united in a partnership. The employer puts into the concern his money, his business experience, and often the exacting and exhausting work of management. The employed puts into the concern his labor. With this joint stock, affairs are carried on. Throughout society we find this partnership of capital and labor, of employer and employed. Without it, large operations are impracticable. Now, it is clearly the true policy of partners to cooperate cordially, and to work together harmoniously. If they become suspicious or antagonistic, their mutual prosperity is inevitably impaired. The wise course, then, for employers and employed is to settle differences about wages, working hours, and all other matters growing out of the relations of capital and labor, by intelligent discussion, friendly consultation, and mutual concession, each side having regard to the rights of the other. The fatal course is for one partner to organize opposition to another. Strikes are as disastrous in practice as they are unsound in theory. Their enormous wastefulness is proved by frequent examples. They involve the idleness of workingmen for days and weeks, and sometimes for months. While thus idle the laborer is receiving nothing, but is consuming his hard-earned savings. He may console himself with the idea that he is supported by some "Society," but that is a delusion, because the funds of the Society are the product of the laborer's toil. Even if the points on which a strike is made be carried, it usually costs more than it is worth. The employed are at a disadvantage with the employers in a strike, because while the employer may lose tens or hundreds of thousands of dollars by the suspension of operations, he is not like the employed, deprived of daily bread for himself and family. Combinations of capitalists for the purpose of crushing labor, and combinations of laborers for the purpose of crushing capital, are alike unwise and immoral. Let the prudent workingman beware of strikes, which are usually instigated by lazy vagabonds who, unwilling or unable to support themselves by skillful and industrious labor, seek to live on the proceeds of noisy and demagogical agitation.

source 19

Meeting Capital on the
Threshold of Its Aggressions

J. M. Campbell

> Compare this emotional appeal for a national strike fund with the
> attitude of the Locomotive Engineers in Source 18, and the prag-
> matic defense of carefully executed strikes in Source 20.

MR. J. M. CAMPBELL then rose and addressed the Convention as
follows:—

MR. PRESIDENT:
I arise to address this Union upon one of the most important measures that has ever been the lot of a trades association to consider—a
measure pregnant with blessings and good to the craft if adopted, but
big with disaster and weakness if allowed longer to continue in its present dormant condition. Your Committee, after careful and prolonged
deliberation on the important measures contained in the able address of
your President, have reported favorably on the National Fund Law, as
a measure wise in its inception and good in its scope of action and
practical uses. It is such a measure as has been wanted in organized
typographical labor for lo! these many years. A measure calculated to
give to our National organization, and particularly to our local Subordinate Unions, that power which of right and of necessity they should
have, and the only power which arrogant capital in the hands of some
unscrupulous possessor will respect—the power of money. An organization like ours, Mr. President, to be respected, and to be enabled to carry
out its purposes, must have the power to enforce its decrees; it must have
at its command the sinews of war in lavish abundance. If it has not this,
it has to bow at all times and under all circumstances to the behests of

International Typographical Union, *Proceedings* (1867), pp. 62–63, 65.

men who would fain render the condition of the skilled laborer but little above that of the serf, with the advantage, perhaps, all on the side of serfdom. How any man of the intelligence a printer is necessarily supposed to possess can vote against the adoption of this most important measure, I cannot for the life of me see. How any man can be so blinded to the wants of the trade, and to the antagonistic circumstances which have always characterized the existence of labor and capital, is a problem I cannot unravel. Capital is and always will be aggressive, and unless means are adopted to resist this aggression, the cause of labor will go down. It is the aggression of capital on labor which compels the English miner to bury himself down, amid the primeval formations of the earth fathoms deep beneath the moaning sea, to dig and delve in poverty and squalor, in ignorance and brutality, that his lordly master may become rich and "lard the lean earth" as he moves along; it is this aggression that harnesses the male and female to the miner's cart, and compels man, formed upright in the image of his Maker, to take the place of the beast of burden. It is the aggression of capital upon labor that compels the printer to remain in the office hour after hour unoccupied, and without the privilege of leaving it; it is this aggression that compels the printer, in many localities, to work for prices which do not yield him a living for himself and family; it is this aggression that introduces into the printing business, wherever it has the chance, apprentices to drive out and reduce the labor of the journeymen; it is this aggression that has sought to introduce female labor to the ruin of male labor. Capital is active, at times unscrupulous, and always exacting to the uttermost its pound of flesh. How is this aggressive encroaching spirit of capital to be met? How does the experience of a century tell us it has been met successfully? Is it by remaining unorganized and poor, and throwing ourselves upon the justice of captial and asking it to hold off its hands, and allow us to enjoy *some* of the rights which nature and nature's God designed that all men should share? Is it by meeting capital with hat in hand and bated breath, and asking it in the suppliant and humble tones of the menial addressing the superior to grant you as a great favor that which you should assert as a great right? Or is it by meeting capital on the threshold of its aggressions, with defiant eye and uplifted hand to strike it down if it dares to intrench upon the dignity or the reserved rights of labor? This aggressive and labor debasing spirit of capital has to be met by organization and money. The mechanic, poor, unorganized and pleading for his rights, is a different man and treated in a different manner from the same man, powerful, backed by a national organization and a national fund, and demanding, not begging for his rights. The single stick and the bundle of sticks is a good illustration of the condition of organized and unorganized labor, and the same bundle of sticks tied with a thread of cotton and a band of steel will serve to illustrate the difference between organized labor without money, and the same labor backed by a sufficient fund to bid defiance to the assaults of capital.

•   •   •

. . . It is a perfect instrument, and if carried to its legitimate consummation, will prove the sheet anchor of our safety. I can understand, Mr. President, why large Unions, like Philadelphia and New Orleans, should not be enthusiastic in a desire for its adoption. They are, perhaps, powerful enough, in the present condition of trade, to protect themselves. But let the small Unions fall, as they have wherever attacked from the want of means for defence, and what becomes of the strength and power of either New Orleans or Philadelphia? They are gone, Mr. President, as the sunlight drinketh dew. This measure will benefit all Unions, because it will give all the same strength and force. Nashville cannot be attacked without New York feeling, and adding her strength to the defence. San Francisco cannot be assailed without Columbia, South Carolina, bearing her brave Palmetto into the fray. It makes us a band of brothers—fulfills the measure of the motto *multum in parvo*, and enables us to say to capital thus far shalt thou go and no farther. Mr. President, I could go on showing the benefits of this measure until both the Convention and myself should tire, but I think I have said enough to convince most that it is our only ark of safety from the storms of capital.

source 20

Avoiding Unsuccessful Strikes

Adolph Strasser

> The selection is from a speech by the President of the Cigar Makers'
> Union, Adolph Strasser. It is a fine statement of the strike policy
> that the great majority of the A.F.L.'s affiliates ultimately adopted.

To the subject of strikes I have devoted considerable time in trying
to investigate the causes of success and failure, and my report on this
question will be more extended than usual.

Much as we may regret the recurrence of these periodical strikes,
I do not know of any remedy that will enable us under present conditions to dispense with them entirely. Judging from the past we will
have strikes in the future. Such being the case it will be your duty
to surround the organization with such safeguards as will limit strikes
to the lowest possible number, and prevent the hasty and impulsive ones.

THE CAUSE OF UNSUCCESSFUL STRIKES

I have tried to investigate, with the limited information at my
disposal, the causes which led to the failure of the largest and most ex-
pensive strikes, both of England and America, and have come to the
conclusion that the lack of success is due to three chief causes:

I. The want of thorough organization, or a loose system of organization.
II. Insufficient funds to meet all requirements.
III. Insufficient knowledge of the conditions of trade, and the in-
auguration of strikes during the most unfavorable season.

Cigar Makers' International Union, *Proceedings* (1885), pp. 3–5.

The last cause, "insufficient knowledge of the conditions of trade," has been the stumbling block in the path of success, both at home and abroad, and rendered futile the efforts of the most powerful organizations.

It is the least understood, and generally recognized when all hopes of success have vanished.

In the October *Journal* of 1882 I have published an article under the caption, "When to Avoid Strikes," which is as true to-day as it was three years ago, and from which I will quote the following:

> Strikes are good when they succeed, but bad when they fail. To know when to strike and when not to strike, is something which requires more than the experience of a few months or a few years in Unionism.

We should avoid strikes at times when trade is declining and the unemployed are on the increase. We should avoid them in places where we have many members not entitled to benefit, and have made no provision for them before the strike is inaugurated.

·   ·   ·

I will now quote from my reports to the several conventions, which will show you that the line of policy I recommended from time to time, was that which rendered success almost positive, inasmuch as it tended to prevent the errors of the past, not only in our own, but also in other trades.

In my report to the Buffalo convention in 1879 I said:

> A variety of opinions prevail in our organizations as to the utility of strikes as one of the means to improve our condition. Some are opposed to strikes on account of taxation; others consider them injurious to the trade; while others again are of the opinion that they indicate a mode of warfare belonging to the past, and therefore threatening to be a failure in the future. I claim that numerous strikes are a sign of the want of proper organization in the trade, and the only remedy against their frequent recurrence is to adopt measures which will bring our organization to some degree of perfection. In the war between the capitalist and the laborer, even in private life, the weak

is attacked by the strong one; it is therefore our duty to introduce such elements of strength into our Union as will command the respect of the employers. Once they know that we are strong, able to battle with them, they will hesitate and consider twice before they risk a defeat.

The old strike laws have exerted a demoralizing influence in every direction. Every local Union claimed to have a legal right to strike whenever they felt aggrieved; and the Executive Board has been considered a mere machinery of approbation, whose duty it was to levy assessments without asking any further question.

No advice was heeded whether it was the proper time to strike or not. Some Unions are laboring under the mistake that every reduction must be resisted without one moment's delay whatsoever, no matter whether there be any prospects of success or not. A dull season and lack of organization are of no importance to them. They allow their members to rush out of the shop without any knowledge of the conditions of trade by which they are surrounded, and will not hesitate although other strikes may occur at the same time in various places. If this suicidal policy should be tolerated in the future, and I trust it will not, the time may not be distant when we lock ourselves out in so many places at one and the same time, that disastrous defeat will surely follow.

In my report to the Chicago convention, in 1880, . . . under the heading of strikes, I said:

> We do not court, nor do we favor them. They should not be resorted to unless all peaceable means have been tried and exhausted. To go out on strike without cool and calm deliberation, where all chances are carefully taken into consideration, is neither heroic nor worthy of imitation. The object of every well regulated union is to check and discourage frequent difficulties; to secure an advance of wages whenever the condition of trade is favorable, without the expedient of a strike.

Two Arguments for
Producers' Cooperation

These two extracts were written over a decade apart, and they indicate the basic and continuing arguments upon which the campaigns for producers' cooperation rested.

CAPITAL IN THE HANDS OF THE MANY

Pittsburgh Advocate

Workingmen and workingwomen must understand and preach to the present and rising generation the great truth that the only way by which the toiling millions can protect themselves from the unjust claims, and soul-crushing tyranny of capital, is for themselves to become capitalists, and all that is necessary to become capitalists, is to save the profits made on what they buy, and on what they produce; and, further, that this saving can be brought about by means of co-operation, and by no other means. . . .

The securing and concentrating of capital is a great blessing, if rightly used.

There is nothing in the hands of man so powerful for both good and evil as money. It is the wrongful use of it which produces nearly all the misery which we see, and it is only by commencing to use it properly that this widespread misery can be done away with, and a better day for labor made to dawn.

We therefore rejoice to see these efforts put forth in favor of a system which justly places capital in the hands of the many under conditions which secure all the advantages of concentration to be used in the interests of the many—the elevation of all and the oppression of none. . . .

Reprint of an article from the *Pittsburgh Advocate* as found in the *Workingmen's Advocate* (August 25, 1866), 1.

But bright as that would be, in a monied point of view, it is nothing to be compared with the good that would result from the improved social, intellectual and moral advancement of the people. Every step in their co-operative career would be educating and elevating in all these respects.

CONFIDENCE IN THEIR OWN CLASS

Charles W. Pope

There is one great truth in national economy that the working people, as a class, do not apparently understand: It is that no considerable improvement can take place in their circumstances as long as they remain simply wage workers. The truth of this assertion can be readily seen when we remember that wages never, in any country, permanently remain above the amount which may be necessary to provide the laborers with those things without which, from long use, they consider it impossible to exist. So long as the producers receive but a portion of their earnings in the form of wages they cannot expect to rise above their present condition, for it is simply impossible. The remedy for this is in their own hands—by becoming their own employers. By this means alone can they secure the full reward of their industry, receiving not only the usual rate of wages, but the entire profits rising therefrom. In the United States of America the working classes are in a position to put this system of self employment into practical operation on the largest scale. They are the possessors of adequate pecuniary resources, of a high degree of intelligence and of great mechanical skill. Many of them possess the necessary ability to fill the position of 'Captains of Industry.' All the conditions necessary to success are in their possession but one, and that one, candor compels me to say, they do not possess. It is confidence in their own class. For instance, it is a fact, as a rule, they will rather deposit their savings in a rotten bank, to be manipulated by men whom they do not know, than loan themselves, on the best security, to people with whom they meet in the everyday walks of life.

Charles W. Pope (Secretary, Shoe Makers' Union of San Francisco), *Labor Standard* (Fall River) (September 3, 1879), 1.

Wage Serfs

Jesse H. Jones

Equity was a "Christian Reform journal devoted to the discussion of the Labor Question." Its editor was the Reverend Jesse H. Jones, a Congregationalist minister who was deeply involved in preaching and working for Christian communism. Jones looked forward to a restoration of the communism of the primitive Church in an American setting. He thus regarded the growth of the industrial order in the United States as a disaster. Although Jones' plans received little support, his antipathy to the industrial system, and its consequences for workingmen, was a basic element in the reform thought of the period.

Some months since we spoke of certain wage laborers as having organized themselves into "a caste of serfs." As the phrase seems to have been misunderstood, we will endeavor to explain it.

All persons of full age who work for wages are by that very fact made to be wage-serfs. No wage laborer can be a freeman. He is dependent upon another for his livelihood; and this fact makes him a bondman to that other. Now if any one does not see this we will not attempt here to prove it. To us it is as clear as geometry. When any body of wage laborers, accept, or seem to accept, their wage condition as permanent, and organize themselves as wagemen to contend with their employers as capitalists, without the distinctly announced purpose to end their wage condition, they do thereby organize themselves into "a caste of serfs," and the step they thus take tends to make them such forever. This is a bitter word to say to American citizens who have supposed themselves free born; but better wormwood now, than wormwood and gall and unremovable chains by and by.

• • •

Equity, II (May 1875), 16.

The only *Christian* method of action would be this. First wage laborers should unite themselves into a Christian brotherhood, solemnly covenanting to have full charge of all of each others' material interests. Then they should declare themselves Christ's freemen, and announce to their employers that they would no longer work with them, except as equals and shareholders. If this should be refused, they should at once withdraw from their employment, and if necessary make arrangements to leave that place, and go where they can be independent. It is inconsistent with Christian freemanship for any man to work for wages for any body.

We do not use this phrase "caste of serfs" for the sake of hurting, but for the sake of those to whom we apply it. The wage classes must come to know their condition, abhor their condition, and revolt from it, before they can be made free.

source 23

The Conflict over Political Action

> The first selection is from a letter sent to the President of the Workingmen's Assembly by William Sylvis in his capacity as President of the National Labor Union. It should be compared with the second selection, which is drawn from a letter sent to the President of the Workingmen's Assembly by H. J. Walls, Secretary of the Cincinnati Trades Assembly. Walls had proposed that the trade unions set up a new national organization to replace the National Labor Union. The two extracts illustrate the sharp conflict within organized labor over political action.

A REMEDY THROUGH THE BALLOT BOX

William Sylvis

I have long since come to the conclusion that no permanent reform can ever be established through the agency of Trade Unions as they are

New York State Workingmen's Assembly, *Proceedings*, V (1869), 28.

now and have been conducted. They are purely defensive in character, and experience has taught us all who have been for any considerable time connected with them, that to keep them alive at all, requires a continued struggle and a vast expenditure of time and money. The organization I have the honor to represent [Molders' International Union] has spent money enough within the past ten years to have effected an entire revolution in our monetary affairs, and secured whatever Congressional legislation we need. Within the ten years mentioned, we have spent a million and a half of dollars, and to-day we have the same struggle to maintain ourselves we ever had; and there will be no end to it until the Workingmen of our country wake up to the necessity of seeking a remedy through the ballot box. All the evils under which we groan are legislative; that is, they are the result of bad laws, and there is no way to reach the matter and effect a cure but by the repeal of those laws, and this can only be done by political action.

THE NEED FOR POLITICAL EDUCATION

H. J. Walls

[Political action] can never take place under the present National Labor Union because it has ceased to be an organization in which all Trade Unionists or workingmen generally can be represented: first because the Constitutions of all Trade Unions prevent them as Unions [from] taking any part in partisan politics; and second, without such a restriction in their Constitutions, their membership being composed of all shades of political opinion, an attempt to force or commit all to one way of acting politically would inevitably result in the destruction of Trade Unions. . . .

From the foregoing it may be inferred that I am opposed to separate political action on the part of workingmen. This would be a mistake. It is because I favor this separate political action, and because I desire the success of such a movement when made, that I now favor the formation of a National Trades' Assembly. Without a thorough organization it is useless to talk of political action. Workingmen who

New York State Workingmen's Assembly, *Proceedings,* VII (1871), 83–84.

have not been made to see the benefits to accrue to them by a union with others of their own trade or calling, or who cannot be held together in Trade Unions, would be but poor material out of which to organize a political party having for its object to almost revolutionize the existing condition of affairs as represented by capital and labor. Men who during the past ten years have resisted all appeals to connect themselves with Trade and Labor Unions will not be likely, at the behest of a few of the members of said Trade Unions, to cast aside their political prejudices and, through the medium of the ballot box, assist in securing to labor that for which Trade Unions were organized and have for years been trying to secure. The workingmen of the country are not educated up to that point. They must be organized, educated and drilled; the wrongs they are laboring under they must thoroughly understand and appreciate, and this cannot be done by announcing the formation of a political party. When the masses are organized as hereinbefore stated— when they, as a mass, appreciate their condition and its remedy—a political party will come of its own volition. The attempt to force an unnatural growth will be a failure.

source 24

These Men Are Not the Robbers

George C. Ward

> The distinction made in this selection between legitimate and oppressive profits was a basic feature of Populist thinking in the 1890's, and it was a major element in the concept of a producing class.

Legitimate profit does not rob labor, because it only secures "fair wages" to industrial managers or "exploiters" of labor. . . .

• • •

Locomotive Firemen's Magazine, XVII (July 1893), 576–77.

Take a "boss" or employing carpenter, painter, blacksmith, printer, tinner or a small storekeeper who hires or does not hire one clerk or more, if such employer or storekeeper does not make more than a decent, comfortable living out of his business or employment, it is clear that he does no injustice to any one and robs no man. . . . The vast majority of our employing managers of productive, distributive and repairing or embellishing industries only manage, by dint of hard work, energy and prudence, to obtain a fairly decent and comfortable living and many thousands of them annually are pressed to the wall, fail in business and lose the small capital they had invested. Very few of them, if any, accumulate any wealth, and they are numbered with the 12,350,000 families, who own, upon the average, $1,255 to each family, and not with the 250,000 families who possess upon the average, $186,000 to each family. Rent, interest and the profit that robs the wageworker, in like manner robs the great bulk of employers and small storekeepers. These men are not the robbers, but should be classified with the robbed, in which category they undoubtedly belong. Until the great middle class realizes and appreciates this fact, Labor can hardly hope to be emancipated from industrial serfdom.

Where then shall we look for the factor profit which robs labor? I will tell you. Look to the vast manufacturing establishments which after paying salaries to managers, heads of departments and foremen, after paying interest upon borrowed capital or bonded indebtedness, yet pay goodly dividends to a multiplicity of stockholders who, performing no labor about the establishment, yet hold shares of stock representing, in most cases, more than the actual value of the plant. Look in the direction of the forty-three listed trusts in the United States, with a gross capitalization of $1,352,700,000, of which $380,000,000 is water. And yet this list does not include some of the largest and most greedy trusts in the country, because no trustworthy information concerning their capitalization can be secured. Look in the direction of the street railway, water, gas and electric light companies and many other kinds of corporations, which are bonded for all or more than they cost, and yet pay, in addition to the interest on the bonds, good, fat dividends upon a capitalization as great in amount as the bonded indebtedness. These are the profits which rob and oppress all productive and distributive labor and play an important part in the concentration of wealth in the hands of the few and the absorption of the total net annual increase in wealth.

Reforming the Currency

National Labor Union

> The program of the National Labor Union rested upon the work of
> Alexander Campbell and Andrew Cameron, the influential editor of
> the *Workingmen's Advocate*. Trade union leaders were never whole-
> heartedly in favor of this program, even during the post-Civil War
> depression. However, monetary reform did attract some prominent
> labor leaders, as well as those reformers who hoped to solve the
> "labor question." By 1870, the reformers dominated the National
> Labor Union, and this selection provides a fine statement of their
> views.

. . . [W]e insist that . . . there shall be issued . . . as the
exclusive circulating medium of the nation, *paper currency made a
legal tender in the payment of all debts, public and private, duties on
import included, and declared the lawful money of the United States,
and convertible at the pleasure of the holder into government bonds,
bearing an interest of three per cent. per annum, payable in lawful
money. The bonds to be likewise convertible into this lawful money at
the option of the holder.*

This system is adapted to the theory of our institutions—sovereignty
in the people—and in harmony with the letter and spirit of our organic
law. It will furnish a circulating medium possessing uniform value,
and will perform all the functions of money, coextensive with the juris-
diction of the law, better than gold, because more convenient; it will
be self-adjusting, and furnish a currency with the necessary flexibility.
It must be evident that under this system the currency can never be so
contracted as to produce a *panic,* and never so expanded as to cause
depreciation. It will be just in its bearings on all classes and interests,
simple in its working, and can be instituted and managed without the

National Labor Union, *Address to the People of the United States on
Money, Land, and Other Subjects of National Importance* (1870), pp. 8–10.

aid of bankers and cunning financiers. Being under the direct control of the people, they will be enabled to prevent the high and fluctuating rates of interest and the violent expansions and contractions of the currency which have caused the monetary crises and commercial revulsions which have heretofore so frequently prostrated all legitimate enterprise and productive industry, deranged commerce, lowered the standard of commercial integrity, and made us little less than a nation of gamblers. It will likewise enable us to effect the equitable distribution of the products of industry and enterprise between capital and labor, thus removing the necessity for the excessive toil which is now over-taxing the mental energies and physical powers of the producing classes, and afford them the time and means requisite for social enjoyment, intellectual culture, and moral improvement.

Its effects in a philanthropic point of view would be equally beneficial. Praiseworthy as are the efforts of the benevolent individuals and societies for the relief of the destitute and suffering and the improvement of the condition of society, they can at best afford but partial relief and effect but temporary improvement. These evils are too general and widespread to be removed by individual or local society efforts. Justice to labor will do more to relieve the destitute, prevent crime and pauperism, enlighten and elevate the masses, and improve the public morals, than all the temperance and other benevolent institutions ever established. It will likewise confer greater benefit on the emancipated slave than all the freedmen's bureaus and aid societies ever instituted. This subject has, then, paramount claims on, and should command the careful attention of, every true philanthropist and Christian. If we would save men's souls, we must first save their bodies.

Finally, important as this subject would be in an economical and philanthropic point of view, it would not be less desirable as a political measure. It would encourage and quicken productive industry in all departments of useful labor, establish equitable commercial relations between all parts of our common country, develop and harmonize that mutuality of interest which naturally exists between the different sections of our extended domain, growing out of varieties of climate and production, which by unwise legislation has been made to appear adverse and conflicting; it would interest each citizen pecuniarily in the preservation and perpetuity of the government, dispensing its blessings impartially to all; it would make us a homogeneous family of States—one in interest, one in sympathy, one in purpose. United by these strong ties, our Union would stand proof alike against the machinations of enemies within and the assault of foes from without.

source **26**

The Effects of an Eight-Hour Day

George Gunton

> This selection states the official policy of the A.F.L. Its reliance upon the ideas of Ira Steward is obvious; in fact, Steward had been a close personal associate of Gunton in the late 1870's. Gunton was a self-educated British immigrant, who came to America in 1874 as a weaver, but soon became involved in union activities and labor reform. He became editor of the *Labor Standard* of Fall River, Massachusetts, in 1878, and through the 1880's he was a prominent spokesman for organized labor's views, especially on the hours question. However, after 1890, Gunton lost favor with labor leaders as he concentrated his attention on the desirable results of the protective tariff and the consolidation of industry into trusts. He increasingly gave up his contact with the labor movement in favor of new friendships with leading politicians and businessmen. Union leaders bemoaned the loss of men like Gunton to more lucrative careers in government, politics, journalism, or business.

HOW AN EIGHT-HOUR SYSTEM WOULD AFFECT WAGES

The adoption of an eight-hour system would tend to increase wages in two ways: first, by reducing enforced idleness; second, by creating new wants, and raising the standard of living. The immediate effect of the general adoption of an eight-hour work day would be to reduce the working time of over eight million adult laborers about two hours a day. This would withdraw about sixteen million hours labor a day from

George Gunton, *The Economic and Social Importance of the Eight-Hour Movement*, A.F.L. Eight-Hour Series, No. 2 (Washington, D.C., 1889), pp. 13–15.

the market without discharging a single laborer. The industrial vacuum thus created would be equal to increasing the present demand for labor nearly twenty per cent. In other words, without increasing either our home or foreign market, but simply to supply the present normal consumption, it would create employment for two million laborers, which is nearly equal to seventy per cent. of the total number of able-bodied paupers and unemployed laborers in America, England, France and Germany. In thus eliminating enforced idleness it would remove the first great obstacle to industrial reform and social progress.

Again, the employment of two million of new laborers would necessarily tend to increase the number of consumers, and thereby enlarge the market for commodities to that extent. That such a result would tend to increase wages is very clear. Although wages would not necessarily rise in the same proportion that enforced idleness is reduced, all the influences would be in that direction. It is a law in all nature that the power of primary forces increases directly as the opposing forces are reduced. Since enforced idleness is the most powerful obstruction to a rise of wages by removing the unemployed, the direct influence of the social forces which tend to promote the rise of real wages would be increased.

Manifestly, therefore, the immediate effect of the adoption of this measure would be to remove the greatest obstacle to industrial peace and progress, and prepare the way for increasing the natural influences which tend to enlarge the general consumption of wealth and raise wages.

The second effect, which would be more gradual, permanent and far-reaching in its nature than the first, would be the result of the increased leisure and social opportunity upon the social character and consumption of the masses. With the removal of enforced idleness, and its degrading influences, over eight million laborers would leave their work each day less exhausted, mentally and physically, and have two hours more leisure. This would mean so much positive opportunity for family life and for general social intercourse, and in a much fresher and more cheerful mood. With increased leisure and less exhaustion, the laborer will be continually forced or attracted into new and more complex social relations, which is the first step toward education and culture in the broadest and deepest sense of the term. In short, it means his gradual introduction into a new social environment, the unconscious influence of which would necessarily awaken and develop new tastes and desires for more social comforts. He would naturally begin to desire more wholesome and better appointed homes, more literature, entertainment, and a greater amount of general social intercourse, not to speak of the intellectual, moral and social improvement that would necessarily result from such conditions. The purely economic effect of this would be little short of revolution. In proportion to the frequency and extent with which the new desires were gratified, the development of which no power on earth could prevent, would they crystallize into urgent wants and necessities. The satisfaction of these would soon become an essential part of the standard of living demanded by the social character and habits of the people, and therefore would make a general rise of real wages inevitable. In fact, these are the only kind of influences which ever did, or ever can, permanently increase the general rate of real wages. This increased consumption and rise of wages means enlargement of the home market, and thereby making a greater concentration of capital and the use of wealth-cheapening machinery possible.

* * *

WOULD A RISE OF WAGES INCREASE PRICES?

It is commonly assumed that every increase of wages must be accompanied by a rise of prices. This is a fundamental mistake that is demonstrated by all the facts of industrial history. The last fifty years, which have witnessed a greater rise of wages than all the rest of the world's history have shown, have also seen the greatest fall of prices ever known. Whether a rise of wages will involve an increase of prices depends entirely upon how the advance of wages is brought about. If wages were arbitrarily increased without any change in the standard of the laborer's living, and the consequent increase in his general consumption, of course an advance of wages would increase the cost of what he produced. But this is entirely different when the rise of wages comes from the natural consequence of a higher standard of living, and a larger general consumption. The larger the market the lower the price, is one of the best established principles in political economy as well as one of the best attested facts in industrial history.

The successful use of improved machinery, which is the only means of permanently reducing the cost of production and lowering prices, is impossible without the use of large capital and extensive production. It is equally true that the concentration of capital and extensive production are compatible only with large aggregate consumption of wealth, which nothing but a high standard of living can sustain. Therefore, whatever tends to raise wages through increasing the aggregate consumption of wealth, necessarily tends to reduce the cost of production and lower prices. This explains why the comfort and luxuries of life are cheaper in England now, with labor at five shillings a day, than they were in the middle ages with labor at less than six pence a day, and why wealth can be produced cheaper in America at two dollars a day than in China at ten cents.

NOR WOULD IT TEND TO REDUCE PROFITS

The idea that an increase of wages involves a diminution of profits is a part of the same heresy which teaches that a fall of wages produces a rise of [profits]. To begin with, the capitalist is not concerned so much about the *rate* as he is the aggregate *amount* of profits he will receive. What he really wants is not so much a large proportion as a large actual amount of wealth; nor has the laborer, or the community so much interest in reducing the actual income of the manufacturer as they have in increasing their own. This can only be economically accomplished by increasing the aggregrate consumption. Low wages make small consumption and a limited use of capital with slow methods of production inevitable, which, even at a high rate of profits, makes a large aggregate income impossible. . . .

We are therefore warranted in saying that the economic effects of a general reduction of the hours of labor would be to raise the standard of living and increase real wages; promote the concentration of capital; and the use of improved machinery; will cheapen production, lower prices, and while diminishing the *rate*, will increase the aggregate *amount* of profits. Obviously, therefore, it would tend to improve the economic and social condition of the laborer and the consumer without injuring that of any other class.

Guaranteeing a Minimum Wage

Massachusetts Bureau of Labor Statistics

> This is one of the earliest statements favoring a minimum wage for all workers through government action. The issue divided reform forces for decades since many who favored extensive regulation of the conditions of labor for women and children were unwilling to accept direct control of the wages of adult men. The question was not resolved until the New Deal's legislation in the 1930's.

Let us revert, at first, to our assertion in the introduction to this part, that "it seems natural and just that a man's labor should be worth, and that his wages should be as much as, with economy and prudence, will comfortably maintain himself and family, enable him to educate his children, and also to lay by enough for his decent support when his laboring powers have failed."

Much can be rightfully and truly said, as we have shown, against the prevailing wage system, but the iconoclasm that strives to break it down, unless at the same time it shows the superstructure of a more equitable and easily managed one, will be devoid of fruitful results or permanent benefit.

We have here, no plan to bring forward as a substitute for the wage system, but only a recommendation, which, if adopted, would reduce by one the list of its weak or criminal acts.

We believe that there should be a certain minimum yearly or daily rate or wage paid for competent adult labor, and that all employment, temporarily, or as the result of contracts, for a less sum, should be discountenanced by public opinion, and, if persisted in, to the detriment of any, should be prevented by appropriate legislation, rigidly enforced.

Massachusetts Bureau of Labor Statistics, *Annual Report*, No. 6 (1875), pp. 445–49, *passim*.

This may seem a chimerical way of treating the wage problem, a direct contravention of the law of supply and demand, a premium upon [a] poor class of labor. But let us examine the matter more closely, and see if what we ask is more than the system should do, to secure what is "natural and just" to the recipients of wage, and if it is not something that can be done without any great violation of the present laws of production.

Such an opinion or law would not say that inferior labor should be paid as much as a better class; it would only provide that a working-man, with a family to support, should receive enough wage to enable him to do it prudently. It would prevent a discontented feeling with regard to all laws, make many more hands self-supporting, and remove many [as] a burden and demand of pauperism upon individual charity and the similar provision made by the state.

*   *   *

Why, in justice, should the broken merchant receive the benefit of the bankrupt law, when unable from loss or poor management to pay his bills, and the broken laborer, no more criminal or lacking in good intentions than the merchant, have only the poor debtor's oath to relieve him (and then only from arrest, the debt remaining), with its attendant stultification of his feelings of manhood?

*   *   *

Firms and corporations, when threatened with loss, reduce expenses, stop manufacturing and, if necessary, pay half the amount of their bills and begin afresh. The workingman suffers by the suspension of work, can not reduce his expenses materially, gets in debt, has no royal way of beginning again, but must keep on with his load of debt still hanging to him. Either one thing or the other, it is plain, should be done. Either every competent adult laborer should receive enough as wages (the minimum sum and as much more as he can command) to enable him to get along without debt, or he should have the same recourse to a relieving-law that merchants, corporations or other employers possess.

How would this minimum wage plan work? The young unmarried workman, with small expenses, would save money, if prudent; when married, he would have something to begin on. His wages, never running below his expenses, would enable him to maintain his independent position. An advance would be made for one child, then for the second and third, providing him with the means for their support and education. At the proper age, he could give to the state healthy workers, both in body and mind. And what would the state have done for him? Simply provided that his return for labor should pay for his living, and that of his children—the latter, in turn, adding to the productive power of the state.

Suggested Readings

The success ethic is thoroughly examined in Irvin Wyllie, *The Self-Made Man in America: The Myth of Rags to Riches* (New Brunswick, N.J.: Rutgers University Press, 1954). See also John Cawelti, *Apostles of the Self-Made Man* (Chicago: University of Chicago Press, 1965); and Richard Mosier, *Making the American Mind: Social and Moral Ideas in the McGuffey Readers* (New York: Kings Crown Press, 1947).

The literature on specific immigrant groups is extensive. Some works that are particularly relevant to our concerns are Theodore Saloutos, *They Remember America: The Story of the Repatriated Greek-Americans* (Berkeley, Calif.: University of California Press, 1956); Moses Rischin, *The Promised City: New York's Jews, 1870–1914* (Cambridge, Mass.: Harvard University Press, 1962); Carl Wittke, *The Irish in America* (Baton Rouge, La.: Louisiana State University Press, 1956); Marcus Hansen, *The Immigrant in American History* (Cambridge, Mass.: Harvard University Press, 1940); Oscar Handlin, *The Uprooted* (Boston: Little, Brown & Company, 1951); and Rowland Berthoff, *British Immigrants in Industrial America, 1790–1950* (Cambridge, Mass.: Harvard University Press, 1953).

The sociologist has given considerable attention to social mobility, including methodological problems, long-term developments, and contemporary trends. Some of the more valuable works in this field are Seymour Lipset and Reinhard Bendix, *Class, Status and Power* (New York: The Free Press, 1953); and *idem, Social Mobility in Industrial Society* (Berkeley, Calif.: University of California Press, 1959); Robert Merton, *Social Theory and Social Structure* (New York: The Free Press, 1957); Richard Centers, *The Psychology of Social Classes* (New York: Russell and Russell, 1961); and Ely Chinoy, *Automobile Workers and the American Dream* (Garden City, N.Y.: Doubleday & Company, Inc., 1955). An interesting attempt to examine mobility as a basic factor in American development is Rowland Berthoff's "The American Social Order: A Conservative Hypothesis," *American Historical Review*, LXV (April 1960), 495–514. Many articles have appeared in sociological journals on aspects of social mobility. See particularly the *American Journal of Sociology*, the *American Sociological Review*, and *Social Forces*.

The study of mobility in the nineteenth century is much less complete than work on the twentieth century. Some of the reasons for this are discussed in Stephan Thernstrom's basic work, *Poverty and Progress: Social Mobility in a Nineteenth-Century City* (Cambridge, Mass.: Harvard University Press, 1964). Other important books are E. P. Hutchinson, *Immigrants and Their Children, 1850–1950* (New York: John Wiley & Sons, Inc., 1956); David Brody, *Steelworkers in America: The Non-Union Era* (Cambridge, Mass.: Harvard University Press, 1960); Vera Shlakman, *Economic History of a Factory Town: A Study of Chicopee, Massachusetts* (Smith College Studies in History, XX, 1934); and Sam Warner, Jr., *Streetcar Suburbs: The Process of Growth in Boston, 1870–1900* (Cambridge, Mass.: Harvard University Press, 1962). Also of interest are Thomas Mayer, "Some Characteristics of Union Members in the 1880's and 1890's," *Labor History*, V (Winter, 1964), 57–66; and Clarence Long, *Wages and Earnings in the United States, 1860–1890* (Princeton, N.J.: Princeton University Press, 1960).

The response of organized labor to the changing position of the worker is examined in Gerald Grob, *Workers and Utopia: A Study of Ideological Conflict in the American Labor Movement, 1865–1900* (Evanston, Ill.: Northwestern University Press, 1961). Jonathan Grossman, *William Sylvis, Pioneer of American Labor* (New York: Columbia University Press, 1945) is an excellent study. See also David Montgomery, *Beyond Equality: Labor and the Radical Republicans, 1862–1872* (New York: Alfred A. Knopf, Inc., 1967); and James Leiby, *Carroll Wright and Labor Reform* (Cambridge, Mass.: Harvard University Press, 1960). Philip Taft, "On the Origins of Business Unionism," *Industrial and Labor Relations Review*, XVII (October 1963), 20–38 stresses the importance of business unionism in the development of the American labor movement. John P. Hall, "The Knights of St. Crispin in Massachusetts, 1869–1878," *Journal of Economic History*, XVIII (June 1958), 161–175, is significant in several respects, including the discussion of possible research problems that arise in studying organized labor in this period.